SLIFE

SLIFE

What Every Teacher Needs to Know

Andrea DeCapua

University of Michigan Press
Ann Arbor

First paperback edition 2023

Published in the United States of America by the
University of Michigan Press

First published September 2019

Paperback ISBN: 978-0-472-03948-7
Ebook ISBN: 978-0-472-12563-0

ACKNOWLEDGMENTS

As always, I am grateful to my colleague and friend, Helaine W. Marshall, for her inspiration, insights, suggestions, and support for this book and for so much of my other work, too. Special thanks also to Kelly Sippell, without question the best editor an author could hope to work with.

CONTENTS

WHY THIS BOOK? ix

1. **WHO ARE SLIFE AND WHAT MAKES THEM DIFFERENT FROM OTHER ENGLISH LANGUAGE LEARNERS?** 1
What Is Formal Education? 1
When Are ELLs SLIFE? 2
Ways of Learning Continuum: The Heterogeneity of SLIFE 6
Four Essential Guidelines to Help SLIFE Succeed 9

2. **DEALING WITH ASSUMPTIONS WHEN TEACHING SLIFE** 12
Assumption: SLIFE Will Know How to "Behave" In Class. 13
Assumption: SLIFE Work Well On Their Own In Class. 16
Assumption: SLIFE Will Know the Basics of Reading and Writing. 17
Assumption: SLIFE Are Familiar and Comfortable With Decontextualized Literacy-Based School Tasks. 18

3. **THE CENTRALITY OF LITERACY, DECONTEXTUALIZED TASKS, AND CHALLENGES FOR SLIFE** 20
Literacy 21
Decontextualized Tasks and Academic Ways of Thinking 29

4. **THE HIDDEN CHALLENGE OF SCHOOL AND A NEW PARADIGM FOR LEARNING** 33
The Hidden Challenge of School 33
What Do SLIFE Bring to the Classroom? 35
A New Paradigm for Learning: The Mutually Adaptive Learning Paradigm 38

5. **PROJECT-BASED LEARNING** 46
Sample Project Incorporating MALP® 51
Final Reflection 55

APPENDIX: MALP® 57
REFERENCES 59

WHY THIS BOOK?

In the last decade, the world has experienced an unprecedented migration of people from their home countries, much of it due to civil unrest, wars, and natural disasters, as well as economic reasons (migrationportal.org). In 2019, for instance, the United Nations Refugee Agency claimed that there were over 70 million forcibly displaced people worldwide (www.unhcr.org/figures-at-a-glance.html). With such large movements of people, teachers in North America, the U.K., and Australia are finding that they have rising numbers of culturally and linguistically diverse immigrant and refugee populations in their classrooms.

A frequent lament I have heard over the last several decades from elementary and secondary school teachers is that they are increasingly encountering English language learners (ELLs) whom they do not know how to serve. These teachers, regardless of their training and experience, feel overwhelmed and ill-equipped because these students are low-literate, have large gaps in subject-area knowledge, and are unfamiliar with classroom basics. Who are these ELLs that these teachers are referring to? What makes them different from other ELLs?

For most ELLs, the priority is to develop English proficiency; in K–12 settings, the priority is to simultaneously acquire grade-level subject-area knowledge. To better serve these learners, various innovative ESL pedagogies have been designed and implemented (e.g., Echevarria et al., 2016); Honigsfeld & Dove, 2014; Snow & Brinton, 2017; Walqui & van Lier, 2010). Initiatives such as these have helped many ELLs develop the necessary language skills, access grade-level subject-area knowledge, and progress satisfactorily in school. Yet, there are other ELLs for whom school presents additional major challenges. These ELLs are approximately nine years or older and are **S**tudents with **L**imited or **I**nterrupted **F**ormal **E**ducation or SLIFE [note that SLIFE, when used, is plural].

Various other labels have been used to refer to this population in North America, such as underschooled youth (Ruiz-de Velasco & Fix, 2000); Limited Formally Schooled ELLs or "LFS ELLs" (Freeman & Freeman, 2002), Students with Interrupted/Inconsistent Formal Education or SIFE (New York State

Department of Education), and ELLs with limited prior schooling (Ontario School Board). In my work, I have chosen to use the acronym "SLIFE" (e.g., DeCapua & Marshall, 2010; DeCapua et al., 2009. Although this acronym is not ideal, it does serve to identify the particular subset of language learners who differ from other language learners in essential ways related to prior educational experiences. It is also the acronym used by the WIDA (World-class Instructional Design and Assessment) consortium and in several states, including Minnesota and Massachusetts.

SLIFE are usually identified as a separate group, if at all, only from approximately 4th grade or 9 years of age. Identifying students as SLIFE only after age 9, or even older in some U.S. states, may be regarded as arbitrary since students who enter formal classrooms at ages 7 or 8 and have never attended school previously will not be on a par with their peers. In support of a minimum age of approximately 9 for possible SLIFE identification, the argument is that in the early primary grades it is (relatively) easy for students to catch up, since younger students are not as cognitively developed as older students and are building foundational skills and knowledge. Whether or not this is truly the case is not within the scope of this book, which does focus on SLIFE aged 9 and older.

The challenges SLIFE face go far beyond language and content: SLIFE need to develop basic literacy skills and foundational subject-area background, as well learn how to "do" school—that is, to learn how to engage in the discourse and practices of formal educational settings. Few teachers feel prepared to work with SLIFE, and most ESL pedagogical practices are inappropriate and/or inadequate for this population. Because of their limited or greatly interrupted participation in formal education, or even in some cases, no exposure to *any* schooling, SLIFE do not have the literacy skills, grade-level content knowledge, or cognitive ways of thinking required to succeed in school. Nevertheless, these students, who are aged 9 and up, come to our classrooms with great knowledge, skills, and cultural capital, including students who may speak two, three, or even more languages.

As educators, it's important to realize that our pedagogical philosophies, approaches, and practices are influenced by our mindsets and beliefs, which have likely been formed in the context of (Western) formal education and the culture of schooling and that these are not necessarily universal. With that recognition and change of mindset, it is possible to understand SLIFE and adjust pedagogical practices away from a **deficit** approach to one of

difference. Distinctive pedagogical approaches are needed to serve SLIFE while leveraging what these students bring to school. By acknowledging difference, we accept the need to engage in **culturally responsive teaching** and recognize how the prior learning experiences of SLIFE have led to the development of a learning paradigm different from that of formal education.

To this end, it behooves both classroom teachers, as well as teacher educators, to become aware of who SLIFE are, why they are different from other ELLs, and how to address their needs. Helping teachers and teacher educators to do so is the reason for this ebook.

This book is only an introduction and overview to SLIFE. For more information on teaching students with limited or interrupted formal education, see:

- *Meeting the needs of students with limited or interrupted formal education (SLIFE) (2nd ed.)* (with Helaine Marshall and Frank Tang, in press)
- *Breaking new ground: Reaching students with limited or interrupted formal education in U.S. secondary schools* (with Helaine Marshall, 2011)
- *Making the transition to classroom success: Culturally responsive teaching for struggling language learners* (with Helaine Marshall, 2013)
- *Culture myths: Applying second language research to classroom teaching* (2018).

These books provide more details on the topics introduced in this ebook, including:

- identifying ELLs who are SLIFE.
- examining underlying cultural differences impacting ways of interpreting one's world and learning.
- using the culturally responsive model, the **Mutually Adaptive Learning Paradigm® (MALP®),** designed to transition SLIFE and other struggling ELLs to formal education.
- applying a project-based learning approach.

One other book, *Crossing Cultures in the Language Classroom, Second Edition*, co-authored with Ann Wintergerst (2016), although not focused specifically on SLIFE, explores important cultural constructs essential in effective intercultural communication as it applies to the classroom and teaching. As such, it is a useful book for all teachers with culturally and linguistically diverse students.

1. Who Are SLIFE and What Makes Them Different From Other English Language Learners?

> During the third week of school, we had four new English language learners (ELLs) come to our school who were placed in my beginner ESL class. We were working on very basic English. The text had a full-page drawing of a classroom, students entering, and a new student who was being greeted by the teacher with a handshake. On the opposing page were student exercises, such as listening to names and checking the ones the students heard. After some practice on the sounds of the English alphabet, there was a little dialogue for the students to practice asking each other's names and how to spell them. These four students didn't know what to do at all. They couldn't understand the picture or how to do any of the activities. I thought it was a language issue but after a while I realized that it wasn't just language but literacy. They barely knew how to read or write in any language. These students were clearly unlike any ELLs I had ever worked with before.
>
> —Mary Ellen, middle school ESL teacher

Mary Ellen was encountering a subgroup of ELLs—those with limited, interrupted, or in some cases, no prior formal education such as we know it. **Students with limited or interrupted formal education (SLIFE)** [note that SLIFE as used here is plural] have not experienced age-appropriate formal education and, because of their previous learning backgrounds, differ significantly from other ELLs, even those who may come from the same country (Browder, 2018).

What Is Formal Education?

Formal education, also referred to as "Western-style formal education," is the type of education familiar to teachers reading this book and found worldwide, albeit with cultural variations (Grigorenko, 2007):

1. It is systematic and highly organized, taking place in a structured setting with trained teachers and standardized curricula.
2. It clusters students in age cohorts.
3. It demands literacy and the ability to interact with print media.
4. It communicates knowledge as distinct subject areas, with material broken down into units presented in definite sequences.
5. It revolves around scientific, abstract ways of thinking.
6. It uses literacy-based, decontextualized tasks for building and demonstrating mastery.

Formal education contrasts with other types of learning. For example, in some cultures, learning may take place within a religious context in which the primary, and often only, purpose is to read and recite sacred texts. In other cultures, learning takes place informally, where learners acquire skills necessary in their daily lives within the contexts of home, family, community, and work.

When Are ELLs SLIFE?

There are, of course, many reasons why a student might be put into a new formal educational situation. SLIFE, unlike other ELLs, may have never had any education, may have missed years of schooling, or may have been forced to drop out because of war, migration, natural disasters, or cultural, family, or economic reasons. For example:

> Rasha arrived here at age 14. Due to the war in Syria, her education was sporadic. After they were bombed out of their home, the family fled to Turkey where there was no schooling available to Rasha.

Some SLIFE may have attended school, but, unlike other ELLs, their education was not equivalent to what is expected in formal education as we know it. Their classes may not have been held consistently or held only for a few days a week, and students may not have attended regularly. As Juan described:

> I walk long way to school and when my family need me in field I work and no go school. Teacher also no go always when rain or when also need work fields.

The schools may have had limited resources, curriculum may have been non-existent, textbooks may not have been available, and/or learning may have focused on repetition and mimicry. In Benoit's words:

> Until I come here, I never need read, no books, no internet, no nothing to read. School only teacher have book, we copy what he say.

Other ELLs, on the other hand, will have attended schools that offered comparable education systems—that is, formal education—before coming to North America (see Chapter 2 "Assumptions and Teaching SLIFE") for more discussion of what formal education is). This ends up being a significant difference between ELLs and SLIFE: ELLs have a concept of school that is, to a large degree, similar in concept to the formal education in North America and Europe. While some cross-cultural variations exist—such as whether students stand up when a teacher enters a room or whether cooperative learning is the norm, they are relatively minor compared to the prior learning experiences of SLIFE.

Literacy

Marjorie, a high school ESL teacher, was working intensively with one of her students when she had an eye-opening experience about what developing basic literacy skills means for low-literate SLIFE:

> We're working on sight words. Toh Rey reads the first words on the list aloud, including the word "long." A little farther down, he comes to the word *along*. He stops and can't go on. I cover up the "a" and ask him to read the word now. He says he can't. He doesn't know this word. I try to talk with him about letters and sounds: "Every letter has a sound." I show him *long* again and ask him what the sound of the first letter is. He doesn't know.
>
> "You just read this word (as I point to *long*)." And then I point to *along* again and again cover up the *a*: "See, it's the same letter and the same sound. What sound was that? "And around and around we went until I realized that he didn't understand that letters represent sounds or that sounds and letters combine into words. He was just memorizing the words in the order they appeared in the list.

If ELLs have developed literacy in their language, they can typically transfer these literacy skills, regardless of language or writing system, to English. Once someone is literate, they are able to extract and exchange meaning via print. However, most SLIFE, as a result of having had no or only limited experience with formal education, possess low or no literacy skills in any language. Letters, sounds, syllables, words, and sentences can be extremely confusing. Even for those SLIFE with some literacy skills, they find using print as a means of information exchange or knowledge-building demanding. Therefore, in contrast to other ELLs, SLIFE need basic literacy instruction; yet historically, few ESL and mainstream teachers who teach beyond the early elementary level, have received training in this (see in Chapter 3, the section "Literacy").

Subject-Area Content Knowledge

Robert, a seventh-grade math teacher, describes one of his early encounters with a new student, whom he soon realized was a SLIFE:

> Jaime told me that he had helped his mother in the market. I could tell he knew arithmetic in the practical sense because when we talked about prices and money, he would tell me how much he needed to buy say, three oranges, and how much change he would get back if I gave him X amount. But any time I gave him any kind of arithmetic worksheet, no matter how simple, he just stared at it.

Because of their backgrounds, SLIFE generally do not have subject-area content knowledge, and, in fact, are often missing what would be considered **foundational knowledge**. Like Jaime, some SLIFE are able to manipulate numbers when working with concrete objects in a context familiar to them, but not able to do so in ways that teachers often take for granted that students beyond kindergarten or first or second grade would know. Likewise, **everyday knowledge** may be fantastical to their SLIFE. Carmine, a fourth-grade teacher, recounted this incidence from her class:

> Our topic was the solar system and to begin I started with the moon, which I figured everyone would be familiar with. I brought in visuals about the moon, as well as a short video clip of the Apollo 11 moon landing. I thought this would activate background knowledge and would motivate them to learn more about the solar system. Two of my students, both SLIFE, refused to believe that men had landed on the moon. "No possible, Miss, no possible."

As this example shows, these SLIFE did not have the basic knowledge around which she would build her unit and that would spark their interest to learn more. Other ELLs will not necessarily have covered the exact same information in school, yet they will still have learned similar content. Topics such as the solar system, genetics, or algebra are standard in formal educational curricula worldwide.

Here is another example: while ELLs will not have studied U.S., Australian, or Canadian history, they will have studied the history of their country, thereby developing a sense of historical time, another concept that is often foreign to SLIFE. Many SLIFE come from cultures in which the conceptualization of time follows natural phenomena such as changes in seasons and the sun and moon's positions in the sky, a major flood, or a particularly poor harvest. For them, the compartmentalization of events based on dates, around which history classes revolve, and the passage of time (e.g., the historical eras often studied) has little meaning to them (DeCapua & Marshall, 2011).

Maps also present challenges. Along with literacy comes the ability to understand representational texts, or visual images such as drawings, graphs, clip art, and symbols (Altherr Flores, 2017; Marshall & DeCapua, 2013). As teachers, we consider visual images standard tools to help learners process information, but understanding images, no matter how realistic they are, is difficult for SLIFE. Some of the difficulty lies in cultural contexts that are unfamiliar to them; if students have never been in a bank, post office, or hospital, they will have trouble interpreting the contexts themselves that the images represent. A larger issue is that when people have not developed good literacy skills, print and representational images are a "code" in which they are still unskilled and must learn. For someone who has no concept of what a map is, looking at a map of the world is meaningless and appears to be just a random collection of shapes and colors (see, in Chapter 3, the section "Visual Literacy").

Identity as a Learner

A final point here is that SLIFE have not developed **identities as learners**. What does this mean? By the time students enter fourth grade in a formal educational system, they know, more or less, how classrooms are conducted and how to go about learning. This entails knowing things like where to put one's name on a worksheet or the need to sit still at one's desk during a class period, understanding how to engage in classroom tasks, such as matching, sorting, or answering multiple choice or fill-in-the blank questions. All of this is difficult and new to SLIFE, as Rosela, a high school ESL teacher, discovered in attempting a worksheet activity with her students:

> I gave the students a very simple task. They had to match the number with the word. You know, the numerals 5, 10, and so on are on top and the written forms below (*five, ten*), and they have to draw a line from one to the other. The SLIFE didn't understand what they were supposed to do. The idea of drawing this line, matching, didn't make any sense to them.

For SLIFE, most features of school might be new to them. They may not be accustomed to, or understand, the need to attend school regularly. Perhaps they could not attend school when the weather was bad because the roads or paths became difficult or impossible to navigate. Or, attending school may have depended on when the family had the financial means to pay for tuition, class materials, or even a student desk (DeCapua et al., in press). It's also possible that they could only attend school when they weren't needed to help the family, whether in the home or at work, as in Oscar's case:

> My family come from small town. My sisters and little brother no went school because its cost money. You have to buy all, book, clothes, pens. I went because I oldest and boy but when I in middle school I miss too many day because I work with my dad when he need me.

Sitting still for long periods of time at desks is a common problem (DeCapua, 2018b). Many SLIFE were contributing members to the family income, whether by working alongside other family members in the fields, as vendors (selling goods on behalf of the family), taking care of younger children, or engaging in animal husbandry or artisanal tasks. Then, if SLIFE did attend school, classes may have only met two or three times a week for a few hours each time. This is why our expectation that students sit and work at their desks for 30 or 45 minutes (or even longer!) with minimal movement is unimaginable to them and almost impossible for anyone who is not used to doing so (Strauss, 2014).

Ways of Learning Continuum: The Heterogeneity of SLIFE

Because SLIFE is a term used for a very heterogeneous group of learners, it's important to think in terms of a **Ways of Learning Continuum** (see Figure 1.1). The continuum would have those SLIFE who have never had

No formal education	Age-appropriate formal education
Orality—learning through oral transmission	Literacy—learning through the written word

Figure 1.1 The Ways of Learning Continuum
(Adapted from DeCapua & Marshall, 2011; Marshall & DeCapua, 2013)

attended any school and have no literacy at all on one end and ELLs with age-appropriate formal education and literacy on the other (DeCapua et al., in press; DeCapua & Marshall, 2011; Marshall & DeCapua, 2013). In between, but still falling toward the left of this continuum are SLIFE with diverse prior learning experiences.

Where would these students fall on the continuum?

> Divine came to the U.S. at age 15 from the Democratic Republic of the Congo. She had had no schooling in her country and was not able to read or write when she enrolled in high school shortly after coming to the United States. Divine clearly falls to the far left of the Ways of Learning Continuum. In addition to her native language, Kinyarwanda, she speaks Kiswahili.
>
> Sonia went to school through fourth grade in her village school, after which time she dropped out to help out at home and on the farm. Now 14 years old, she registers to attend school and the district has decided to enroll her in eighth grade. Her native language is Spanish.
>
> Ahmed attended school through sixth grade in Syria until the growing civil unrest made going to school dangerous. His family fled to a neighboring country where they lived in a refugee camp with no opportunities for schooling until they were relocated to Canada. At age 16, he was able to start going to school again. His native language is Arabic.
>
> Jairo had three years of schooling in Spanish although he is a native speaker of Mam, an indigenous language of Guatemala. He has basic decoding skills, i.e., he recognizes and can copy letters and words. He is 16 and is now attending high school.

These snapshots of four SLIFE illustrate the heterogeneity in education, literacy, English proficiency, and content-area subject knowledge that SLIFE bring to the classroom, in addition to their different home languages and cultures. While Divine clearly falls to the far left on the Ways of Learning Continuum, followed by Jairo, Sonia and Ahmed who range somewhat closer to the middle (see DeCapua et al., in press, for more discussion and examples). Nevertheless, despite their heterogeneity, these students all share core characteristics that make them different from other ELLs (see Table 1.1).

In summary, SLIFE, unlike other ELLs, come from backgrounds that prevented them from being able to participate in age-appropriate formal education on par as we understand it. As such, SLIFE face formidable challenges. Since SLIFE are language learners, they, like all ELLs need to develop their overall English proficiency, as well as cognitively demanding, age and grade-level academic language proficiency. In addition, and unlike other ELLs, when SLIFE are in formal education classes, they need to:

- simultaneously learn grade-level content knowledge
- gain basic literacy and numeracy skills
- acquire foundational subject-area content.

Less obviously, and yet even more essential, SLIFE need to acquire specific ways of thinking—that is, academic ways of thinking—that are learned through participation in formal education and that will be new, the most part, for SLIFE (DeCapua & Marshall, 2011; DeCapua 2016). These academic ways of thinking are in large part a hidden challenge (see Chapter 4

Table 1.1: Summary: SLIFE versus Other ELLs

Characteristics of SLIFE	Characteristics of Other ELLs
No, interrupted, or limited formal education	Age-appropriate formal education
No or low literacy	Age-appropriate literacy
Missing subject-area content knowledge, even foundational	Age and grade-level subject-area content knowledge
Unfamiliar with how to "do" school	Have an identity as a learner

"The Hidden Challenge of School and a New Paradigm for Learning"). For high-school aged SLIFE, these challenges are particularly daunting since they must develop all of these skills, knowledge, and ways of thinking within the relatively short time frame of high school before aging out (DeCapua et al., 2009; Treschan & Mehrotra, 2013). Many SLIFE enter high school aged 15, 16, or even older, leaving them little time to overcome these challenges and earn a high school diploma before they "age out," i.e., become too old to stay in high school. Although by federal law everyone has the right to a high school education until age 21, few high schools are either ready or prepared to serve older teens. (If students turn 21 during the school year, they can finish out that year.)

Four Essential Guidelines to Help SLIFE Succeed

Since readers are likely primarily concerned with how they can help SLIFE succeed in their classes and in school, four guidelines will be discussed:

- Guideline #1: Question your own assumptions.
- Guideline #2: Foster two-way communication.
- Guideline #3: Explicitly teach school tasks and academic ways of thinking.
- Guideline #4: Promote project-based learning.

Guideline #1: Question Your Own Assumptions.

We all experience difficulties realizing how much our beliefs, values, and interpretation of the world around us are formed by our culture and lived experiences, including schooling. Teachers are both the products and purveyors of formal education and school culture and, as such, have developed specific expectations of what learning and teaching entail. When we encounter students who do not behave and perform the way other students who have had age-appropriate education do, it can be difficult to understand what challenges, beyond language, all ELLs face and how to adjust our pedagogy appropriately. When we work with SLIFE, it is important to need to conscientiously and consistently question our beliefs, perspectives, and priorities about teaching and learning (see Chapter 2 "Dealing With Assumptions When Teaching SLIFE").

Guideline #2: Foster Two-Way Communication.

Learn from your students. This may seem obvious, but often we forget that our students, their families, and community members are those in the best position to help us understand who they are, what their prior life and schooling experiences have been, and what they see as their needs, expectations, and challenges. The fact that, for this guideline, information comes from the students is intentional. Generally, when educators think of communication, it is the school community communicating with the students and their families; the school community initiates explaining the requirements, the paperwork that needs to be completed, what is happening in school, and so on. Here, though, teachers should be listening to the students to actively solicit information from them, their families, their community. When language is an issue, it is essential to identify someone in the community who can serve as an interpreter and cultural broker—that is, someone who understands who your SLIFE are (see, in Chapter 2, the section "Assumption: SLIFE Will Know How to 'Behave' In Class").

An additional point regarding two-way communication relates to trauma. Many SLIFE have witnessed or experienced traumatic events and may suffer from post-traumatic stress disorder (PTSD). Through two-way communication, teachers become aware of who might have PTSD and which classroom topics could be potentially explosive, requiring extra sensitivity, care, and understanding.

Guideline #3: Explicitly Teach School Tasks and Academic Ways of Thinking.

As discussed, the expectations and demands of formal education are largely, if not completely, new to SLIFE. This includes not only subject-area content and basic classroom behaviors, but particular ways of engaging in learning. For example, classroom tasks such as asking students to categorize words, objects, or ideas, are based on specific ways of thinking—academic ways of understanding and organizing the world. This is because these ways of thinking are the ones that are taught and practiced in formal education systems globally and that form the basis of both tasks and ways of thinking for work and life in modern societies (Flynn, 2007). Because these types of tasks and ways of thinking are so pervasive in school and life, we often take them for granted and do not realize that some students need to be taught how to do basic school tasks and how to understand academic ways of thinking (see, in Chapter 3, the section "Decontextualized Tasks and Academic Ways of Thinking").

Guideline #4: Promote Project-Based Learning.

Across grades and content areas, there has been a push to incorporate project-based learning (e.g., Boss & Krauss, 2018). For SLIFE, engaging in projects, rather than the traditional lesson-based approach, is key, as we will be shown in Chapter 5 "Project-Based Learning." In brief, the advantages of projects are that they:

- support the development of all language skill areas in concert with building subject area knowledge and academic ways of thinking
- allow for maximum differentiation to allow for student language proficiency, literacy skills, and content-area knowledge
- are learner-centered rather than teacher-centered, encouraging maximum student engagement and participation.

These four guidelines form the framework throughout this e-book as we explore how teachers can better understand SLIFE so they can provide them with the best possible support as they learn to navigate the unfamiliar world of formal education.

2. Dealing With Assumptions When Teaching SLIFE

> Maria is a former SLIFE that I worked closely with. When I began working with her, she had only basic literacy skills in Spanish; she didn't know math facts or have a lot of content knowledge. My expectations for Maria were very low and I never thought she would make much progress. I've been amazed to see how much progress she has made. She was able to transition into mainstream courses and is about to graduate. Ever since I realized that Maria was making progress, I've had a different attitude toward SLIFE and now set high expectations for all of them.
>
> —Katrina, high school bilingual/ESL teacher

At this point, you may be thinking, "Where do I possibly start? SLIFE can do so little. How are they ever going to catch up?" This is a natural response; however, we need to examine this reaction carefully and consider it in light of the previous chapter's Guideline #1: Question your own assumptions. While it is true that SLIFE may not have a lot of "school knowledge" or understand school culture, they do bring a wealth of knowledge and experience to the classroom. Teachers are unlikely to be aware of what SLIFE know and can do because these are not part of the canon of formal education and it is not similar to what they, themselves, experienced. Of course, today's teachers are concerned about how to meet state curriculum goals and state standards and how to prepare students for mandated standardized tests. All of that is more complicated with SLIFE.

An important piece of teaching SLIFE is to realize that they are not students who are **less than**. This **deficit view** is rooted in the assumptions about formal education: *At this age and in this grade, you should be able to do X, Y, and Z.* But unlike other students, whether ELLs or their other peers, SLIFE have not had age-appropriate formal education. Consider: how can you be expected to know something if you were never taught it? An analogy would be to take a group of say, six teachers from your school—perhaps one each of ELA, math, science, history, ESL, and art—and leave them to fend for themselves in a deserted, isolated area with only an axe, a knife, matches, and nothing else. How well do you think they would fare? How much would their school knowledge help in this type of situation, even if they knew what each item could do? Knowing what a knife can do doesn't necessarily mean someone knows how to use it effectively in this type of situation. Perhaps for some there might be an initial sense of excitement: "Hey, no problem. We can figure this out." Maybe one person in the group has had previous outdoor experience. But, most likely for most put in this situation, the reaction would be one of panic. Not only is this not "glamping," but it is a test of survival, something that most teachers have had no training in. A lack of survival skills, however, does not mean that any of these teachers are "less" of a person; they are just people who have not developed the skills and knowledge necessary for their new reality.

The same is true for SLIFE when it comes to school. They are encountering significantly new ways of thinking, interacting, and doing than they have previously been accustomed to, and they need time and assistance in transitioning to the demands of formal education. If we evaluate SLIFE through the lens or perspective of formal education, it's easy to find them "lacking." However, it is essential that we consider school from their perspective—they have learned in different ways with different expectations.. In so doing, we move away from a deficit view of what SLIFE *cannot* do toward realizing in what ways school and its expectations and demands are all (mostly) new to them.

Keeping Guideline #1 in mind, let's examine some assumptions surrounding formal education more carefully, beginning with school culture. Although we cannot examine every assumption that teachers are likely to hold, even by considering some common ones will clearly demonstrate how the expectations of formal education are not universal and how the majority of these are generally internalized in the early primary years of school.

Assumption: SLIFE Will Know How to "Behave" In Class.

Another assumption is that adolescent SLIFE will know how to comply with common school and classroom procedures and behaviors—that is, aspects of school culture that are learned and reinforced in the very first years of formal education. Here are common procedures and behaviors that can be unfamiliar to SLIFE:

- holding and using a pen or pencil. This includes not pressing too hard on the pencil and repeatedly breaking the point and not pressing too hard with a pen and making holes in the paper.

- writing on the lines and not above, between, or below
- writing one's name at the top right or left side of the page, not just anywhere
- using a keyboard or mouse
- filling in bubbles on scantron answer sheets
- keeping track and organizing handouts, worksheets, and other papers
- needing permission to leave the classroom and only for limited reasons, such as using the bathroom
- having to sit for entire periods at a desk while paying attention to the teacher and to what else might be happening in the classroom. This includes not talking while the teacher or someone else is, nor randomly getting up and moving about, and having to raise one's hand in response to teacher questions
- standing in line at the cafeteria
- needing permission slips (for field trips) and hall passes
- the role and importance of regular attendance, being on time, and grades
- the highly structured school day.

Because SLIFE have had minimal exposure to formal education, they have not been "socialized" to these kinds of typical behaviors, practices, and procedures of school culture. In short, they are learning what it means to "do school" (DeCapua et al., in press; DeCapua et al., 2009). Because SLIFE have not participated fully in formal education and have different—not better, not worse—ways of thinking than what is expected and central to formal education (DeCapua, 2016), in the classroom, they experience **cultural dissonance**, or strong feelings of bewilderment and alienation because their knowledge, skills, and ways of thinking differ significantly from those of formal education. The severity of the cultural dissonance depends in large part on how much formal education they had. For those who have never been to school, learning to hold a writing implement and sitting at a desk for 30 minutes is an accomplishment. Hassan, a nomad in his home country who had no prior formal education, expressed his feelings after his first weeks in a U.S. school:

> We sit only sometimes, we rest, we eat, but on ground or pillow. We always move because always we need to do. For me, very hard sit at desk. And just listen to teacher. And sit.

So how can teachers help someone for whom "school" is a (relatively) new concept? Handing SLIFE printed instructions for them or other family members to read (whether in English or translated to the home language), or reprimanding them when they do not meet expectations or requirements, are not good approaches. When literacy is minimal, print is not an effective means for conveying information, even when written in the native language of SLIFE.

Repeatedly reprimanding—rather than demonstrating—does not address the root cause. When people are unaware of why what they are doing is not appropriate and are not shown the alternative modes, they are less likely to correct their behavior. Consider Chapter 1's Guideline #2: Foster Two-Way Communication. Is there someone, such as a former SLIFE from their culture, extended family members, an aide familiar with their culture(s), or someone in the community who can help the school community understand what factors might be influencing the inappropriate or unacceptable behaviors? Another avenue is to contact professional organizations such as TESOL (Teachers of English to Speakers of Other Languages) at tesol.org, or CAL (Center for Applied Linguistics (cal.org), or non-profits such as the Spring Institute (springinstitute.org), or Welcoming America (www.welcomingamerica.org/learn/resources).

To help alleviate difficulties when sitting for long periods of time, there are a variety of activities that allow student movement, which can also address the issue of cognitive overload (Savina et al., 2016). SLIFE are not only learning a new language, new content, and a new environment, but they are also developing identities as learners, a process that other ELLs have engaged in since their earliest years in primary school. One of the approaches to learning that can help them is a more learner-centered (as opposed to a teacher-centered) classroom. One way to do that is through project-based learning, explored in greater detail at the end of this book.

Project-based learning moves instruction away from a reliance on worksheets, which present an obstacle for SLIFE, given their limited literacy skills and understanding of how to "do" a worksheet. Essentially, worksheets invite passivity because they are a paper to be "filled out" with what the "teacher wants." This mindset tends to lead students to focus simply on getting it completed in any way possible, rather than on processing the concepts underlying the worksheet. (This may be true for other students who are struggling too—not just SLIFE.) In addition, SLIFE are likely, even after extensive review of the written instructions on a worksheet, to turn to the teacher or another student and ask for oral clarification and explanation because they do not understand more broadly what they are supposed to do (DeCapua et al., in press).

Assumption: SLIFE Work Well On Their Own In Class.

Another common assumption is that students are able and willing to engage in classroom tasks and assessments by themselves. When students are given worksheets to complete or questions to respond to, for instance, teachers expect is that each student will do so individually, unless specifically told to work with a partner or a small group. When teachers are evaluating student learning, students are required to take tests and quizzes on their own, without asking for anyone else's help. In other words, teachers assume (and enforce) individual participation and demonstration of mastery on classroom tasks and assessments (DeCapua & Marshall, 2011; Marshall & DeCapua, 2013). This assumption is based on one underlying cultural belief of formal education—the emphasis on individual effort and individual achievement in the formal classroom (DeCapua, 2018a).

Individualism and **collectivism** are terms that describe how people in different cultures identify themselves with respect to others (Hofstede & Hofstede, 2005; Triandis, 1995). In cultures that are more individualistic, the focus is on who a person is as an individual, with strong emphasis on personal self-interest and individual autonomy. In collectivistic cultures, in contrast, the emphasis is on the group rather than the person. People consider the views, desires, and good of their group more important than those of any one individual. They prize sharing knowledge and effort and see achievement as benefiting all members of the group (DeCapua & Wintergerst, 2016). The individualistic orientation is reflected in formal educational systems in countries such as the United States and Canada, which are considered to be individualistic cultures. Although group work and cooperative learning are often encouraged in these classrooms, individual effort, assessment, and achievement remain primary. A common term used in education that readers will be familiar with is **scaffolding**. The idea behind scaffolding is that teachers will first provide the necessary supports that learners need and then will gradually withdraw these supports so that learners can become more independent in their learning (DeCapua, 2018a; DeCapua & Marshall, 2011).

Most cultures, however, lean toward collectivism (Hofstede & Hofstede, 2005; Triandis, 1995), so it is likely SLIFE will come from collectivist cultures and behave accordingly. For instance, the teacher may be talking and notice that two SLIFE are also talking, and then conclude that they are not paying attention. Or, the teacher may view student behavior as disruptive when students are supposed to be working on their own on an in-class assignment and a SLIFE gets up and goes to the other side of the room to be with a classmate.

In reality, what is happening is that the less proficient student is seeking help from a more proficient peer to understand and be able to do the work (DeCapua, 2018b). For SLIFE, working alone and being always accountable for their own work are not situations that they are accustomed to, or that they feel comfortable doing. This collectivistic perspective can be summed up this way: why do something all by myself when we can help each other?

Assumption: SLIFE Will Know the Basics of Reading and Writing.

In the very first years of formal education, students learn the basics: how to form letters, how sounds and letters combine to make words, what syllables are, how to use a piece of paper (which side goes up), and what the pages or parts (title, author, table contents, index, and so on) of books look like. The key point is that knowledge of the basics of literacy are learned at an early age and, if they have not been taught at that time, then students cannot be expected to know them. When low or pre-literate adolescent SLIFE are placed into grades based on age, teachers assume they know such basics. In some cases, it is very likely that they will know these basics, but many will not. This means that teachers of SLIFE find that they are not able to depend on print materials in the same way they would for other learners.

How quickly SLIFE gain literacy depends on many factors. One of these is how far to the left a student is on the Ways of Learning Continuum (Figure 1.1). For Divine, who has had no schooling, even the concept of language as consisting of words, syllables, and sounds (phonemes, phonetics) is challenging; she will need more time than other SLIFE who have more literacy skills. For SLIFE with some literacy, another factor is the writing system. While literacy skills are highly transferable from one language to another, for low-literate SLIFE, whether or not the writing system matches that of English (the Latin alphabet) affects their acquisition of literacy in English. For Sonia, who is a Spanish speaker, the basics will be similar to English because the same alphabet is used in both languages and both Spanish and English are read and written from left to right. For Ahmed, whose native language is Arabic, it will be a completely new alphabet and a different way of reading—not right to left.

And, for all SLIFE, their proficiency in English will influence their acquisition and development of literacy in their new language. The lower their proficiency, the more difficult it is, since they are learning language and literacy skills simultaneously. *Thus, one incorrect assumption is that all adolescent and adult ELLs will know the basics and conventions of literacy in their native language.*

Since SLIFE do not have the literacy skills of their peers in any language, they must be instructed in the basic building blocks of literacy in their new language, English. Phonemic awareness, phonics, fluency, sight words, and text comprehension are pivotal components for constructing meaning from text (Kurvers, 2015). When teaching basic literacy, teachers need to use age-appropriate materials, not materials created for primary grades, which are childish and generally culture-bound. Some useful resources are:

Bow Valley College. 2009. *Learning for life: An ESL literacy handbook.* Available at: https://globalaccess.bowvalleycollege.ca/products-services/practical-guide-teaching-esl-literacy

Literacy Education and Second Language Learning for Adults (LESLLA). Website with resources: www.leslla.org/teacher-resources

Rigor: Language and literacy for older students reading at primary levels. Grade reading series available from Benchmark Education: https://benchmarkeducation.com/teachers/series/rigor/where/language/english

Assumption: SLIFE Are Familiar and Comfortable With Decontextualized Literacy-Based School Tasks.

School-based tasks are those tasks that teachers have students do in order to build and/or demonstrate mastery of knowledge. These are tasks such as matching, sorting, fill-in-the-blank, or multiple choice and true/false questions. As previously discussed, SLIFE do not have the reading and writing skills of their peers, so literacy-based classroom tasks are challenging for them. In addition to literacy, school-based tasks assume that students (1) know how to engage with these types of tasks, and (2) have developed the ways of thinking that underpin performing the tasks.

To illustrate the difficulties beyond language that SLIFE face when confronted by classroom tasks, consider the example of true/false questions, a common assessment task.

For ELLs, these questions can be a challenge because of language and content, but for SLIFE, there is the additional challenge of not understanding their purpose. These questions have little or no purpose for SLIFE. First, they are decontextualized and so have no connection to their lived experiences. Think about it: People do not walk around the world asking other people true/false questions.

These are also confusing from a literacy perspective. SLIFE are just learning to use print as a knowledge source but are now being asked to distinguish between true and false information. "Why do I need to learn what is not true?," they think. Their viewpoint is "Teach me what I need to learn and I will learn it" (Marshall & DeCapua, 2013, p. 19).

Consider this example as a way to help SLIFE understand how to "do" these types of questions (Marshall & DeCapua, 2013, p. 57):

> Begin with simple yes/no questions about the students in the class. Does Carmen have a sister? Does Vuong have a brother? Does Yasmin have a cell phone? The students answer, using Yes or No. The language, content, and how to respond are all familiar to the students. Next. the teacher rephrases the questions as statements and asks the students to respond Yes or No, either orally or in writing.
>
> | | | |
> |---|---|---|
> | Carmen has a sister | Yes | No |
> | Vuong has a brother. | Yes | No |
> | Yasmin has a cell phone. | Yes | No |
>
> Once this activity has been completed, the teacher introduces the terms *True* for *Yes* and *False* for *No,* explaining that these words are the ones commonly used in school:
>
> | | | |
> |---|---|---|
> | Carmen has a sister. | True | False |
> | Vuong has a brother. | True | False |
> | Yasmin has a cell phone. | True | False |
>
> Finally, the teacher introduces new content that the students may or may not know:
>
> | | | |
> |---|---|---|
> | Beijing is the capital of China | True | False |
> | Istanbul is the capital of Turkey. | True | False |
> | Melbourne is the capital of Australia. | True | False |

At this point, students are familiar with the task. The teacher can now confidently say that the response is an indication relating to content mastery and not to the academic language, or the type of task being used to elicit a response. Once the students can readily respond to literal true/false questions, the teacher will need to develop their skills in incorporating higher-level thinking skills into the true/false format.

3. The Centrality of Literacy, Decontextualized Tasks, and Challenges for SLIFE

> We had three new ELLs arrive in mid-October to our high school, It didn't take long for us to realize that they were different from our usual ELLs. They didn't understand what a day schedule was; they didn't know what a locker was, or how to use the combination locks. But the hardest was that they couldn't follow even our most basic ESL text and the teachers in their subject classes said they were "hopeless" because they couldn't seem to do anything or know anything.
>
> —Sharon, high school counselor

What kind of learning experiences do SLIFE come from? SLIFE are a heterogenous group as illustrated by the Ways of Learning Continuum and the four snapshots of SLIFE presented earlier. However, despite the great differences among SLIFE, they all share the fact that, for whatever reason, they were not able to participate in age-appropriate formal education (DeCapua, 2016). Instead, they come from backgrounds of primarily informal ways of learning—that is, learning that takes place within sociocultural contexts of family and community daily living. It is learning that:

1. occurs in response to immediate needs and demands of daily life and centers on pragmatic skills and tasks resulting in tangible results, such as food, shelter, clothing, animal husbandry, childrearing, and so on
2. follows traditional mentoring and apprenticeship models in which learners observe, imitate, receive feedback(much of it via demonstration), and continue through practice until mastery
3. does not require or even use literacy.

This type of learning obviously contrasts to formal education, which:

1. depends on literacy as the means to access and share information and knowledge

2. separates knowledge into subjects, such as math, English Language Arts, or history (Robinson, 2011)
3. features decontextualized school tasks in these subject areas to build and demonstrate mastery, tasks that demand literacy and are based on associated ways of thinking
4. fosters specific cognitive pathways, that is, academic ways of thinking.

Literacy

We begin by examining the centrality of print in formal education. Because literacy is central to formal education, it is seen as the norm. Students who deviate from the norm by not having age-appropriate literacy are frequently assumed to be less intelligent and less motivated to learn. Such judgments fail to take into account that SLIFE have not had opportunities to develop age-appropriate literacy skills.

For most teachers of SLIFE, it can be difficult to relate to struggles SLIFE face in becoming literate because we live in a world dominated by print. Even for those people who don't like to read per se, they still read constantly, whether street signs or text messages, ordering from a menu, following the instructions to pump gasoline, filling out school or government forms, and for all the many other mundane activities that demand literacy. As Bruer (1993) notes, those with good literacy engage in literacy practices with little effort and cannot but help but read the print around them.

Even when SLIFE have attended school previously, they still struggle because they will not be used to or comfortable with the centrality of print in formal education. Lin, a high school social studies teacher, sums this up briefly in describing one of her students:

> Chen had literacy, but he'd missed a lot of school before he came here and he found navigating print materials challenging. In his regular [content-area] classes, Chen would stare at the same page of the textbook the whole time or sleep at his desk because it was all beyond him. He told me that he didn't know how to read a map. There were too many words on that map and most of them new words to him.

Developing literacy skills is neither easy nor natural, even for young children in their native language. SLIFE are not young children; by most definitions, they are age 9 or older, and come to formal classrooms as competent speakers of at least one language, many with knowledge of multiple languages.

> Before I learn read and write, I look in paper or sign and see thing but no see letters, words, just thing.
>
> Khalid, middle school SLIFE from Yemen

> I learn alphabet in my language [Spanish]. Easy read word but read no understand more long sentence or story.
>
> Ester, high school SLIFE from Mexico

What SLIFE have not yet developed, or are in the initial stages of developing, is print literacy. We can think of literacy skills as a set of tools to exchange knowledge, to communicate, and to demonstrate learning (Meltzer et al., 2002). Literacy demands the mobilization of highly specialized and interacting skills and techniques to produce meaning in ways significantly different from spoken language.

Reading, as expected and utilized in formal education, is more than just decoding. Reading is an active cognitive process that takes place primarily in the mind. Language and thought interact to derive meaning from words, sentences, and longer narratives (Grabe & Stoller, 2011). For SLIFE new to print like Khalid, learning the English alphabet and sound-letter correspondence and the concept of syllables, words, and sentences are initial hurdles. Others, like Ester, will know the basics but now must learn them in English and go well beyond decoding skills. At the most basic level, literacy entails understanding and gaining skills in:

- the English alphabet
- the concept of sound-letter correspondence, as well as the irregular sound-symbol correspondences in English
- word segmentation into syllables
- how combinations of letter strings become syllables and words
- the print representation of phrases, words, sentences, and longer text
- comprehending, not just decoding (i.e., reading without understanding) text
- connecting oral language to print.

To expand, developing literacy skills in English requires:

- **orthographic knowledge**, or sound-letter correspondence. English is not a one-to-one system. There are 26 letters in the alphabet, but many more sounds. Thus, the phonemic representation of a letter in the context of a word differs from how it sounds and how it may be written. Compare, for instance, the *a* in *mat* versus the *a* in *mate* or the *o* in *rod* versus the *o* in *rode.* Here the addition of the *e* at the end of the words has changed the vowel sound. Likewise, a sound may be represented by different letter combinations. The sound *f* is written differently as *fig, tough,* or *photograph*; the sound *ch* can be written with these same letters—*church, chocolate*—or be represented in other letter combinations such as *question* or *furniture.*

- **phonological awareness**, which is the ability to interpret letters as sounds, to recognize how combinations of letter strings become syllables and words, to know which words share a common sound and which sounds rhyme (or don't), and to identify syllable boundaries in words.
- **phonemic awareness**, which is the ability to understand how individual speech sounds combine to form words and phrases, to break a word into individual sounds (segmenting), and to say a word after hearing the individual sounds (blending). For example, *fish* consists of three individual sounds *f*, short *i*, and *ish.* These are blended to produce *fish.*

Few teachers, whether ESL or mainstream, have been trained to teach emergent literacy skills, that is, the basics of reading and writing, to adolescents who are at the same time learning a new language, English. Moreover, SLIFE who range close to the left end of the Ways of Learning Continuum will need generally need time and practice to develop literacy because they have a longer journey than those who had more formal education. For all SLIFE, there are several crucial aspects teachers need to be aware of, to develop an appropriate mindset about SLIFE and literacy:

- SLIFE may not have developed an understanding of sound-to-letter correspondence, syllable breaks, words, and phrases because they have not learned how to "take apart" language and will need to be introduced to these concepts. For SLIFE, language represents a tool for oral communication, not a system of individual pieces. Understanding what a syllable is can be as difficult for these students to understand as the concept of a sentence as something that consists of separate words that have different functions (e.g., subject, verb, noun). See Bow Valley, 2009 and leslla.org for suggestions and resources.
- SLIFE with no or very low literacy process oral language differently. Their literacy level, for example, affects their ability to recall and accurately produce or modify corrective feedback (Tarone et al., 2007).

- Because they are developing literacy in a language new to them, they may not be able to distinguish sounds and sound clusters of English that are different from those in their language.

The tendency for teachers is to start with print materials, such as worksheets. Students are often given worksheets with drawings and given such tasks as circling the initial middle, or final sound they hear. These materials are confusing for SLIFE with their backgrounds in informal ways of learning; they tend to prefer spoken language to exchange information and knowledge. In addition, many SLIFE, as we saw with Hassan, are accustomed to actively doing something. Thus, teachers must carefully use the oral to scaffold print, and think in terms of hands-on learning activities. While it is not in the scope of this ebook to delve deeply into teaching literacy, here are some general suggestions.

For SLIFE first learning to write, the tasks of forming letters, combining them to write words, leaving spaces between words, staying on the line, and using correct punctuation are arduous and require much time and practice (Burt et al., 2003). Some tips to help students are:

- Ask students to practice tracing letters with their fingers before trying to write them.
  - Make sure they do not attempt too many letters at one time.
- Provide lined paper such as that used in primary grades to practice forming letters.
- Give multiple opportunities for continual repetition and practice. Learning to write takes time.
- Introduce computers and tablets early on. While these do not teach SLIFE handwriting skills, they do allow them to produce text sooner than doing so by hand.
- At every class session, write the day and full date on the board as you say it. Ask the students to read it using the sentence frame, both individually and as a class:

  Today is ____. (Today is Friday, April 26, 2019).

  Once students are comfortable doing this, do the same with the previous day and next day:

  Yesterday was ____. (Yesterday was Thursday, April 25, 2019). Tomorrow will be ___ (Saturday, April 27, 2019).

- Find or take photos of objects familiar to the students.

  - Show the photos and say the names.
  - Write or project the names of objects on the board and show the matching photos.
  - Practice the words.
    - Read chorally.
    - Pair match sets of photos with the names of objects.
    - Students copy the names of their items into their notebooks or vocabulary books.

As an expansion:

  - Ask students to sort the photos by initial or final sounds.
- Assign students to create *collages* of photos from magazines or of their own drawings for sight words or words with certain sounds, such as consonant clusters or long and short vowels.
- Prepare *sentence scrambles* by cutting up sentences and tasking students with putting them together. Sentence scrambles teach sentence organization, grammar, and punctuation as students evaluate which pieces belong in which order. Be sure the sentences are familiar and do not introduce new vocabulary or grammatical structures.
- Engage in **Total Physical Response (TPR)**, which connects body movement with language learning (Asher, 1982).
  - To introduce TPR, the teacher can say and simultaneously perform a few simple commands such as "Stand up" or "Sit down."
  - The students listen, watch, and imitate. The teacher repeats the commands without movement to be sure the students understand.
  - Next, the teacher writes the commands on the board and, while pointing, the class reads them together orally.
  - Later, students receive slips of paper with the commands, must read them, and act out the command.
  - Once the students have grasped TPR, different actions are introduced.
- Play games such as Flyswatter and scavenger hunts.
  - *Flyswatter.* The teacher randomly writes words the students have been learning on the board, divides the class into two teams, and gives each team a fly swatter (or something like it). As the teacher calls out a word, team players take turns racing to hit the word first. The team to "swat" the word first wins a point.

  - *Scavenger hunts*. The students look for objects in the classroom or school that begin with the same sound or letter as their first name. Or, students can have a list of sounds and look for objects with the same initial letter.

- Embrace the **Language Experience Approach (LEA)** (Nessel & Dixon, 2008). In LEA, the aim is to jointly create texts based on a shared experience.
  - Begin by establishing a shared context, such as listening to a story, watching a movie, or going on a field trip.
  - Next, together with the students, produce text about this shared experience. This piece of writing can be short or longer depending on the literacy of SLIFE. Write the sentences or phrases generated by the students on the board.
  - Correct the text as necessary, type it up, and make copies for the students.
  - This text then becomes the focus of a variety of literacy activities, ranging from forming basic sentences to practicing basic reading skills to learning how to create cohesive passages (DeCapua, 2018a; DeCapua et al., in press; Marshall & DeCapua, 2013).

LEA also encourages Guideline #4: Promote project-based learning.

Visual Literacy

When teaching SLIFE, what you as a teacher may think are givens will often not work with SLIFE. Part of developing literacy skills with SLIFE is making them comfortable with and able to benefit from print materials, including visual representations. Do not assume SLIFE will understand visual representations. Visual literacy—that is, the ability to interpret charts, tables, maps, drawings, and graphic organizers—is a type of literacy critical to success in school for which SLIFE will need explicit instruction. For example, worksheets and drawings are generally confusing to SLIFE who are developing initial literacy skills. Common clip art of such items as a pen or drawings of people doing things may be incomprehensible to SLIFE (Altherr Flores, 2017), I have observed classrooms in which more literate SLIFE were working with popular low-level ESL writing texts that used abstract or cartoon-like drawings of events and places as writing prompts. Even these students were confused as to what the pictures were supposed to represent, especially when they depicted scenes outside their realm of experience, such as the Miami skyline, a European café, or opening a checking account.

To better understand the issue of difficulties of visual representations for low-literate SLIFE, consider how frequently graphic organizers are used as an effective scaffolding technique. But what if you have not seen anything like this before? Becoming literate changes the architecture of the brain and how people frame the world (Ardila et al., 2010). Print is a two-dimensional world, one significantly different than the real, concrete world of lived experience. The ability to interact with and exchange information via the written word is one thing, but being able to interpret visual representations such as drawings, images, graphs, and symbols is another; these types of visuals are abstract two-dimensional representations that require understanding a "code."

For SLIFE like those in Altherr Flores' study, who fall toward the left end on the Ways of Learning Continuum, only the actual item ("realia")—that is, the object itself—will have meaning for them (Williams & Chapman, 2007). SLIFE will need explicit guidance in how to use the various visual representations as they move from understanding tangible objects to processing words and graphics as representations of things, and later, concepts (DeCapua et al., in press).

Various activities can help SLIFE make the transition from the concrete to the abstract. Here is one step-by-step example that can be modified as needed:

1. Bring in real objects such as an apple, a pen, or a glass filled with water. Ask students to look at them, touch them, and pick them up.
2. Show the students black-and-white photographs of the same items, and ask them to place the photos next to the actual items.
3. Do the same thing with color photographs.
4. Once the students are comfortable with matching the items with the two types of photos, show them various drawings of the items, identifying which item each drawing represents.
5. Ask the students to sort each item with all its depictions, e.g., place together with the apple the corresponding black-and-white photo, the color photo, and the drawing.

DeCapua and Marshall (2011) describe an expansion of this step-by-step process in the Collections project, one purpose of which is to transition SLIFE to increasing abstraction of the real and concrete. A sequence of exercises is described that begins with a real item, in this case an apple, and a collection of items that are apple-shaped like the real item, such as a potholder, a nightlight, a teapot, a keychain, a paperweight, and so on. These exercises are designed to shift ways of thinking that are grounded in lived experience to abstract, formal academic ways of thinking. Note that the Collections project also illustrates Guideline #4, Promote project-based learning.

Returning to graphic organizers, these can be introduced in a number of ways, depending on the type of organizer. Sequencing organizers, for instance, can be tied to food chains familiar to students, e.g., wormàfishà-people or grassàcowàpeople. Here the students can order the objects (either photos or plastic replicas) of what eats what and then enter the information into a graphic organizer. Sequencing graphic organizers can also be practiced through the creation of a timeline of significant personal events, e.g., student's date of birth, date of arrival into this country, date when first started school, and so on. While there are no visual objects, the facts are highly relevant to the students.

Another common visual representation is the use of speech bubbles, which are often initially puzzling to SLIFE. One way to break this down for SLIFE is to do the following:

1. Prepare in advance:
   - a simple, short dialogue, e.g. My name is ____. Her/his name is _____.
   - name tags with your students' names, as well as one with your name.
   - two speech bubbles with sentence frames from your simple dialogue. This can be done on small handheld erase boards or something similar, as long as students' names can be added and changed.
   - two generic drawings of heads (non-gender specific) with speech bubbles.
2. Ask students to put their name tag on their chests. Do the same with yours.
3. Orally model and act out your dialogue: (pointing to yourself) My name is ____. (pointing to the next person) Her/his name is ____.
4. Ask students in a round robin format to do the same.
5. Take the two dry erase boards with the speech bubbles and ask for a volunteer to work with you in front of the rest of the class.
6. Keep one dry erase board, add your name and the volunteer's name to the sentence frames in the speech bubble.

7. As you hold your speech bubble, read the sentence dialogue as you point to each word and students follow along. Exchange roles with the volunteer and do the same again after you have altered the names.
8. Give students the generic drawings of heads and speech bubbles and have them practice with each other saying the dialogue and using the speech bubbles.
9. As a follow-up, students can find speech bubbles in other printed sources, such as in an ESL text, to see how they are being used.

Note that this activity also practices the use of a blank line ____ as indicating that here students are supposed to add information and/or text.

By providing explicit support of the three-dimensional world of real objects to the two-dimensional world of literacy and print, teachers are following Guidelines #1 and #2. They **realize their own assumptions** about teaching and learning do not necessarily apply to SLIFE. Rather than expecting that SLIFE will understand diagrams, drawings, and other visual representations, teachers are prepared that this may be new to them. They are **fostering two-way communication** by "listening" to their students, in that they observe student behaviors in order to be able to modify and instructional practices accordingly. When teachers see SLIFE struggling, they work with them to understand what they find difficult about the print: is it the language, the content, or might it be the visuals themselves?

In working with SLIFE and keeping in mind their low literacy, some essential practices are in Table 3.1.

Decontextualized Tasks and Academic Ways of Thinking

As discussed, school-based tasks are those tasks that teachers have students do in order to build and/or demonstrate mastery of knowledge. Not only do these tasks require literacy, but students must (1) know how to do these tasks, and (2) have developed the types of cognitive pathways—that is, the academic ways of thinking associated with a given tasks. Decontextualized tasks include:

- matching
- sorting
- fill-in-the blank
- labeling

Table 3.1: Essential Literacy Practices

Avoid	Try Instead
overwhelming students with too much paper and print, whether worksheets, texts, etc.	keeping print materials to a minimum, particularly for low-literacy SLIFE. Include real objects, photographs, video clips, and other digital visual and audio media to supplement print text.
relying on worksheets or texts with drawings, especially ones that do not indicate they have been designed for SLIFE.	• using text and worksheets with minimal and larger-sized print font and with colorful photos directly related to the text. • using real objects or color photos when introducing the alphabet and phonics to represent the sounds first. Be sure students will recognize the vocabulary items you are using to represent sounds and letters. If they have never seen a kite, vest, or yo-yo, these examples are not likely to be useful.
depending exclusively on commercial textbooks and readers	working with student-created materials for literacy development as much as possible. This can include • creating simple class books (see Marshall & DeCapua, 2009) • personal stories using the Language Experience Approach (see also DeCapua & Marshall, 2011; DeCapua et al., in press; and project-based tasks • longer theme booklets (see Marshall & DeCapua, 2013) looking for commercial textbooks or readers that include clear color photos and high-interest, age-appropriate content. Establish a reading corner with basic readers, including ones in their home languages if possible, that students can check out and read on their own.

- completing and/or interpreting graphic organizers, tables, charts, graphs
- true/false questions
- multiple choice questions.

For SLIFE, a crucial hurdle to developing literacy skills is learning to engage in the types of tasks and associated academic ways of thinking demanded in formal education (DeCapua & Marshall, 2011; Marshall & DeCapua, 2013). To illustrate the difficulties beyond language that SLIFE face when confronted by classroom tasks, consider the example of true/false questions, a common assessment task. For all ELLs, these questions can be a challenge because of language and content, but for SLIFE, there is an additional challenge of not understanding their purpose. These questions have little or no purpose for SLIFE. First, questions and tasks need both contextualization and need clear connections to students' lived experiences. Think about it: people do not walk around the world asking each other true/false questions.

As discussed earlier, tasks like true/false questions, that are unrelated to students' real-world experiences, are also confusing from a literacy perspective. SLIFE are just learning to use print as a knowledge source but are now being asked to distinguish between true and false information. Again, why do I need to learn what is not true, they think. Their viewpoint is: "Teach me what I need to learn and I will learn it" (Marshall & DeCapua, 2013, p. 19).

Let's take an example of a common decontextualized task, multiple choice questions, which are particularly popular on standardized tests. Imagine you are taking a standardized, multiple choice test. In your mind, picture four objects: an axe, a log, a hammer, and a saw. Now comes the test question:

Which item does not belong?

a) the axe
b) the log
c) the hammer
d) the saw

(Luria, 1976)

To answer this question correctly you need not only literacy and language, but you also have to understand what the test question is asking you to do—namely, realize that this is a test of whether or not you know how to *classify*. Of the four objects, three of them can be classified as "tools." Only the log does not fit in this class. Some of you may have thought to yourself, "I'm going to choose c) the hammer. It doesn't belong because I can use the axe and the saw to do something with the log." From a functional perspective, this is certainly true and the answer SLIFE are most likely to choose based on the same mental thought process. However, even if you did choose c) the hammer, after our discussion, you as a teacher can see why this is the wrong answer from the perspective of what the standardized test question is actually testing—not language, not content, but an academic way of interpreting the world. Academic ways of thinking are not rooted in real-world experience but derived from abstract concepts, such as classification based on specific identifiable characteristics. In this example, these characteristics are those that determine what makes a tool and that thereby exclude b) the log. This explanation is not likely to be accepted by SLIFE who see the world pragmatically—what objects can be used together with what other objects—and which eliminates in this case the c) hammer.

The concept of classification is initially taught in early childhood through shape sorters and other educational toys and activities, and children gradually become more sophisticated in their thinking about classifying as they progress through grades in school (DeCapua & Marshall, 2011). SLIFE are new to this type of formal analysis and teachers cannot expect that their SLIFE will already know how to classify items, as expected in formal education. The ability to apply the concept of classification—and all of the other academic ways of thinking—to the content in each of the school subjects is essential to school success. SLIFE need to begin with the notion of identifying categories, a less academic way of thinking about grouping items, and then move into the concept of classifying them. (For additional discussions of decontextualized question, suggestions for helping students learn the tasks and associated academic ways of thinking, see DeCapua, 2018b; DeCapua & Marshall, 2011; DeCapua et al., in press; DeCapua & Triulzi, in press; and Marshall & DeCapua, 2013.)

4. The Hidden Challenge of School and a New Paradigm for Learning

> After working with Javier for a while, I realized that it was so hard for him to acquire new vocabulary and access academic content because of his lack of exposure to things we take for granted. He didn't know what a post office, postage stamp, or letter was, had no concept of money. One day he became all excited because the class was talking planets, something he thought he knew all about from movies. What he had a lot of trouble with was understanding that there are real planets in the sky—that those dots in the sky at night, the stars, are planets—but not like *Star Wars*.
>
> —Anysa, ESL co-teacher, middle school

The Hidden Challenge of School

SLIFE face obvious challenges related to school behaviors, language, literacy, and content knowledge, but, as we will explore here, there is also the hidden challenge of academic ways of thinking. These ways of thinking are "hidden" because, although they are an integral part of education and daily life in the developed world, they are largely invisible.

Consider this example (DeCapua & Marshall, 2011, pp. 41–42): Ms. Zukowski was working with her middle school SLIFE on foundational math and geometric shapes. After the class had reviewed the vocabulary, she gave each student a bag with various shapes in different colors. She instructed the students to take the shapes out of the bags, sort them, and place them in the appropriately labeled (round, square, etc.) boxes on her desk. After a few minutes, Ms. Zukowski realized that the students were sorting by color and not by shape.

Ms. Zukowski thought it was "obvious" that this activity was based on sorting by the shared characteristics of the shapes: triangles have three sides; circles are round, and so on, so they all "belong" together. It did not occur to her that the task—sorting by shape—would pose a problem for students at this age. For the SLIFE, however, color was salient while shapes were not. While we understand that sorting by color is done under other circumstances, perhaps organizing clothes or thread or yarn, these are functional approaches. What Ms. Zukowski was expecting was the "school" or scientific approach that even very young kids learn in pre-school—that is, categorization or classification based on shared characteristics as defined by scientific modes of logic and reasoning (Flynn, 2007). This illustrates how academic ways of thinking underlie the daily tasks we do in school and in life without necessarily realizing it. Remember that familiarity with decontextualized school tasks, no matter "how basic," and the associated academic way of thinking cannot be assumed (see Marshall & DeCapua, 2013, for additional discussion and examples). It is important to remember that SLIFE can and will engage in academic ways of thinking if taught how to do so.

Ms. Zukowski used physical objects, geometric shapes, for the students to sort. There was no worksheet involved and no literacy required. Yet, even so, SLIFE still had difficulty with the task because it required an unexpected academic way of thinking to them.

This example illustrates the need to question assumptions, especially with older SLIFE. Academic or, as Flynn (2007) calls them, "scientific" ways of thinking are learned through participation in formal education as we know it.

Understanding Underlying Ways of Thinking

Teachers reduce the cognitive load by *not* introducing new language and new content at the same time they are building familiarity with tasks and ways of thinking (DeCapua & Marshall, 2011). All too often, SLIFE encounter great difficulties when the task that they are asked to do has three unfamiliar aspects or schemata:

- new language
- new content
- new type of task based on literacy and grounded in a new way of thinking.

To address Guideline #3, "Explicitly teach school tasks and academic ways of thinking," using this example, *categorization* and *classification* are two common academic ways of thinking. For SLIFE new to school, no matter their age, such as those in Ms. Zukowski's class, it is useful that they first build familiarity with categorization before actually engaging in decontextualized school tasks. For example, SLIFE can work on sorting photos of family members, or jobs, or sorting activities they like. Some ideas are:

- Students bring in photos of family members and sort them by age, gender, or other criteria they determine.
- The teacher provides a selection of photos of jobs familiar to the students, and students sort them into categories: jobs done in the home or outside the home, jobs that require special training or tools, or any other categories the students may suggest. (Alternatively, students find photos on the internet for the teacher to print out and use in this activity.)
- The class brainstorms activities that SLIFE and their families like, such as playing soccer or watching movies. The students then practice categorizing them by indoor/outdoor, team or individual, technology required or not, and so on.

SLIFE can work on additional academic ways of thinking by engaging in other school-based tasks that build on these categorization activities, such as

- analyzing results to calculate percentages and entering these into a table
- comparing and contrasting findings in a Venn diagram
- designing graphs of their analyses to display.

As these examples suggest, thinking in terms of projects rather than lessons, is a better approach when working with SLIFE. (See Chapter 5, "Project-Based Learning.")

What Do SLIFE Bring to the Classroom?

Elena, a SLIFE high school student from Mexico, says:

> Teachers never ask we know about. We studying America history, we learning about Mexico and Mexican people in old U.S. but teacher never ask nothing about Mexico to me even though me, I from Mexico! And Juan, Lupe, and other student too.

SLIFE do not come to formal education as blank slates; they bring a wealth of knowledge and experience to the classroom, which teachers can and should leverage. In addition to making curriculum and content more meaningful to the students, honoring, respecting, and incorporating their knowledge and experience helps move teachers away from the deficit view of what SLIFE can't do or don't know to a "difference" view.

To start, it's important for teachers to understand who their SLIFE are as people, not just as students in their class. While close relationships between ESL teachers and their students are common, this is not generally the case with content-area teachers—keep in mind Guideline #2, "Foster two-way communication." Generally, the school communicates with students and their families, in terms of informing them about what they need to do and describing school policies, requirements, programs, and deadlines. In two-way communication, in contrast, SLIFE, their family members, relatives, religious leaders, and other community members become resources for the school community to hear the voices of SLIFE and have meaningful dialogue (see DeCapua & Marshall, 2011; Marshall & DeCapua, 2013, for more discussion). By listening to these other voices and acquiring greater insight into SLIFE and their lives, teachers can be better equipped to tailor learning to student needs.

Some ways teachers and the school community can foster two-way communication (Guideline #2) are:

- Promote cultural exchanges where SLIFE and their community share information. These can range from informal meet-and-greet coffee get-togethers to participation in faculty and staff professional development training to exchange historical, religious, geographical, and cultural information.
- Enlist people fluent in the language(s) of SLIFE and English who are familiar with and can explain critical elements of culture, particularly where instances of culture clash are likely to occur (see DeCapua, 2018a, and DeCapua & Wintergerst, 2016, for discussions of critical cultural elements).
- Hold school conferences and meetings outside the school, such as in community centers, with translators as necessary. Meeting in places other than the school can be easier for family and community members to get to, feel less threatening, and encourage greater participation and engagement in meaningful dialogue.
- Wherever and whenever meetings are held, provide refreshments. Even just water and store-bought cookies create a welcoming atmosphere (DeCapua et al., 2009).

When teachers truly understand their students as people, they are able to tap into their "funds of knowledge" (González et al., 2005). **Funds of knowledge** refers to the cultural backgrounds, life experiences, and knowledge that SLIFE bring with them to school. Because these are outside the curricula of formal education, this knowledge is not recognized or valued (DeCapua, 2016). Many SLIFE have had what we would consider adult responsibilities for many years, such as caring for younger family members at an early age even when they themselves are only four or five years old, or being active participants in the economic well-being of their families also at a very early age.

Through identifying and building on students' funds of knowledge, teachers assist in reducing cultural dissonance and transitioning SLIFE to formal education. For example, in a U.S. history class where the curriculum required covering the U.S. Civil War, Ms. Anton related aspects to students' lives—what they liked to do in their free time—to what the soldiers did in their free time (DeCapua & Marshall, 2011). One student discovered that some soldiers enjoyed whittling and became excited because he too whittled, a skill he had learned from his uncle. Ms. Anton encouraged him to bring in some objects he had whittled and, for the first time, this SLIFE found himself able to share something the other students found remarkable. Even though whittling was not related to the curriculum, it became the "hook" that Ms. Anton was then able to use to motivate him to engage in the class.

Note that Guideline #2 is additionally important in allowing teachers to identify SLIFE who experienced trauma and could potentially have strong emotional reactions to particular curriculum topics. For example, learning about the U.S. Civil War could precipitate adverse reactions among SLIFE who themselves have experienced war.

Some common funds of knowledge teachers may want to investigate include:

- home-related activities, such as cooking or bicycle, car, or machinery repair
- handicrafts such as weaving, sewing, carving, or pottery
- agricultural activities such as gardening, planting, or harvesting
- artwork, music, or dance
- family business such as being a market or street vendor
- home improvement, maintenance, and repair
- storytelling
- personal experiences or narratives families can relate to historical events.

The desire to tap into their students' funds of knowledge is not always easy. Teachers must be careful to avoid making false assumptions and overgeneralizations. Here is a case in point: One social studies teacher wanted to involve her SLIFE, who were all from Mexico, by making connections between the Mexican Cinco de Mayo and the U.S. 4th of July Independence Day holidays. In her lesson, she showed a video of dancers in traditional costume performing a dance for Cinco de Mayo and she then tried to initiate a discussion about Cinco de Mayo, but she was met with blank stares. Finally, one student raised his hand and said that they didn't know what this holiday was. These SLIFE came from a southern region of Mexico where this holiday is chiefly unknown because Cinco de Mayo is neither a national holiday nor one that celebrates Mexican independence. It is a minor holiday that celebrates the victory of Mexican forces against the French in the nineteenth century and is primarily celebrated in Puebla, the region where the battle took place. It is a significantly larger holiday (thanks in large part to liquor company marketing) in the United States than in Mexico. In fact, the video the teacher had chosen was of traditional Mexican dancing being performed for a Cinco de Mayo celebration in Denver, Colorado. Although she had good intentions and was trying to help students make connections, she did not know enough about the Mexican holiday, its traditions in Mexico, or her students. Had she started by first eliciting information from her SLIFE about holidays they celebrated, she could have avoided this mistake.

By fostering two-way communication and avoiding assumptions, teachers build relationships with their SLIFE and families and can connect subject-area content to their lived experiences. Hammond (2001), for example, describes a school gardening project that involved students and their families. The teacher leveraged what the students and their families knew about gardening to both the science and math curricula.

A New Paradigm for Learning: The Mutually Adaptive Learning Paradigm

Populations like SLIFE who are not being served by conventional pedagogy benefit from instruction that is culturally responsive. This means that teachers, as well as the larger the school community, must engage with students by first actively listening to, and subsequently to taking action to support students (Gay, 2000; 2018). The Mutually Adaptive Learning Paradigm (MALP®)

(Marshall, 1998) is an instructional model in the tradition of **culturally responsive instruction** as outlined by Gay (2000; 2018). It is *mutually adaptive* because both teachers and students must adapt. MALP® intentionally and selectively combines elements from the learning paradigms of both SLIFE and formal education to decrease cultural dissonance and address the needs of SLIFE. The implementation of MALP® offers teachers a way to teach SLIFE from a difference rather than deficit perspective and actively honors and incorporates the funds of knowledge they bring to the classroom while also transitioning them to the demands and expectations of formal education. MALP® also brings the hidden challenge of school—that is, academic ways of thinking—to the forefront of instruction. The following is a brief overview of MALP®, extensively discussed and illustrated in DeCapua and Marshall (2011) and Marshall and DeCapua (2013).

There are three major components to the MALP® model: Accept Conditions, Combine Processes, and Focus on Activities Using Familiar Language and Content. Each component has two elements (see the Appendix).

Accept Conditions for Learning: Immediate Relevance and Interconnectedness

Conditions refers to what must be present in the classroom for learning to take place, namely immediate relevance and interconnectedness. For SLIFE, coming from informal ways of learning where they learn what they need when they need it, immediate relevance is crucial. Here, teachers find ways to make something in their lesson relate to the lives of their students and not necessarily the curriculum, at least initially. Remember that Ms. Anton built in immediate relevance to the Civil War unit by making associations between the free time activities of her SLIFE and Civil War soldiers.

You will recall that the vast majority of SLIFE come from cultures that are collectivistic. When classroom activities foster relationships among the students, as well as with the teacher, SLIFE come to regard the class as their community and feel a sense of interconnectedness. Therefore, being able to build community in the classroom through two-way communication (Guideline #2) is critical. At the very least, teachers should learn this type of information about their SLIFE:

- places lived
  - Were these rural or urban areas, or refugee camps?
  - What was the geography (e.g., in mountains, near coast, tropical, arid)?

- languages spoken (some may be conversant in two, three, four, or even more languages)
- family constellation
  - Who do they consider members of their family?
  - Who lives here with them?
  - Who is elsewhere? Where?
  - What skills or talents might family members have?
- skills, talents, free time activities.
  - What instruments and sports do they play?
  - What kind of work have they done?
  - What dances and crafts do they know?
  - How do they like spend free time?

In addition, teachers must develop a deep understanding of their SLIFE, one that goes beyond "heroes, holidays, and ethnic celebrations" or the "dos and taboos" of any given culture (DeCapua & Wintergerst, 2016; Ngo, 2010). Unfortunately, understanding a culture is all too often reduced to celebrations about food or overgeneralizations about people from a certain country, such as people from X country always do Y. (See DeCapua, 2018a and DeCapua & Wintergerst, 2016 for discussions and examples of overgeneralizing and cultural stereotyping.)

It's important for school personnel to seek out information about the history (even in brief) about the country and its important values. The more you know about your SLIFE as individuals, the more you will be able to ensure that lessons contain something of immediate relevance from their perspective. Flaitz (2018) and usahello.org, for instance, provide essential cultural information about countries from which many SLIFE come that educators will find helpful. You will also find that students' funds of knowledge are rich resources to tap. This enables you to leverage better what you know about their SLIFE when planning activities to continually build interconnectedness among students.

Combine Processes for Learning: Group Responsibility with Individual Accountability and Oral Transmission with the Written Word

Processes for learning describe how people prefer to access and exchange knowledge and information. SLIFE generally prefer shared responsibility and the oral mode. In formal education, in contrast, individual accountability and the written mode are the norm. To transition SLIFE to the demands and expectations about learning in formal education, their preferred processes must be combined with those of formal education.

The first element of this component is *combining shared responsibility with individual accountability.* It's more typical for SLIFE to be used to learning from others, following a mentoring or apprenticeship approach in which learning is characterized by observation, imitation, feedback, and imitation again, until mastery is achieved (Silva et al., 2010). In formal education, in contrast, teacher-directed instruction, and individual work and individual accountability are the norm. To help SLIFE adjust to working independently and being individually accountable for their work, teachers can allow group responsibility while requiring students to complete some tasks on their own. When one student asks another for help, avoid seeing this as a hindrance to learning and instead as an acceptable practice in certain contexts, such as when students are working collectively on a classroom task. Since SLIFE must learn to work individually, particularly on assessments, teachers can help SLIFE understand when they cannot share responsibility for learning and must do their own work. By fostering pair and group work yet ensuring that at the same time all students must accomplish something on their own, SLIFE learn to move easily between group responsibility and individual accountability.

Ms. Lopez, for instance, would have the SLIFE work on math problems in small groups (DeCapua & Marshall, 2010). Once they had solved the problems, all the students in a given group would come to the board. As one of the group members read the problem out loud to the rest of the class, another student would write line-by-line the solution while still another student performed a check to prove the solution was correct. In this way, although the students shared the responsibility of solving the problem, each one was accountable for presenting an aspect to the rest of the class. To build individual accountability through group responsibility, Ms. Lopez varied how the students alternated engaging in these activities. For example, at times she assigned each student one problem to solve. After they had worked on their problems on their own, the students went up in groups to write their solutions on the board so that they could help each other. The full class then viewed the problem solutions and listened as students took turns presenting their assigned problems and the solutions.

The second element, *combining the oral with the written*, refers to the fact that SLIFE generally prefer to access and exchange information and knowledge orally. Since education hinges on good literacy skills, SLIFE must learn to use print as the desirable medium of exchange, at least in school. To do so, the written language must be continually scaffolded by oral interaction, with explicit connections regularly made from print to spoken language and the reverse (Bigelow & Watson, 2012). This includes pointing to words as the class reads as a group, the choral reading of sentences, and using story-reading bookmarks to help guide students' eyes as they read text (see DeCapua et al., in press; DeCapua et al., 2009).

A creative way to combine the oral and written is through a survey. The example described next formed the introduction to a project on preparing a fruit salad and was designed as both a vocabulary and grammar activity. Through the survey, the students practiced the names of fruits and the grammatical concept of count nouns in the singular and plural (see DeCapua, 2017 for a discussion on count and non-count nouns). Subsequently, the students incorporated the vocabulary and their knowledge of count nouns into their fruit salad project.

1. Bring in photos of or actual fruit, along with index cards with the name of each fruit on a different card. Have more than one of each item ready or photos depicting multiple pieces of the same fruit (e.g., two lemons) but do not share them with the students yet.
   a. As you show the fruit and say its name, write it on the board.
   b. Point, say, and ask students to repeat the name.
   c. Mix up the cards you brought in. Put students in pairs or small groups to match the cards to the fruit or photos, reading each word aloud.
2. Once the students are comfortable reading and understanding the vocabulary, they can practice simple sentences. Introduce the photos depicting multiple pieces of the same fruit that they have not seen yet. Draw students' attention to the fact that they are now looking at multiple items, meaning they now need to use the plural *-s*.
3. Show the single item, say a sentence, write it on the board, and then ask students to practice reading it.

   I have one lemon.
   I have two lemons.
   Continue this with a few more pieces of fruit and move on when students are ready.
4. Pass out the photos with multiple pieces of fruit so that each student has one photo.
5. In pairs, students can practice saying the sentences.

6. They then write the sentences about their fruit, using **sentence frames**, such as

   I have one ___.
   I have two ___.

   Caveat: Don't assume the students will understand how to use a sentence frame with blank lines; they may need first to practice understanding the role of blank lines.

This activity is then expanded so that students can describe their likes and dislikes, such as:

   I like ___
   I don't like ____.

And subsequently, do a simple survey on the board:

   Who likes _____?
   Who doesn't like _____?

7. Tally the students' responses and using this as a guide and then work with the students to produce two model sentences.

   _____ of the students like _____.
   Five students like oranges.
   _____ of the students don't like _____.
   Two don't like cherries.

8. Write a few of these sentences on the board. Practice reading them chorally or have the students practice in pairs.
9. Ask the students to write 1–3 sentences about their likes/dislikes into their notebooks using the sentence frames. Then they practice reading them aloud to a partner.

There are many other ways to combine processes for learning. Ideally, teachers think in terms of projects, rather than lessons (Guideline #4, "Promote project-based learning"). For example, many SLIFE come from rich oral literacy traditions and are skilled at storytelling and reciting poetry, which are often considered performances requiring delivery arts and audience participation at predetermined moments (Finnegan, 2017; MacDonald, 1999). One way to capitalize on this is for a SLIFE with more English proficiency to tell the class a story, which then forms the basis for a class LEA (Language Experience Approach)writing and reading project.

Creating a class poem together is another way to combine the oral and written. There are several ways to start, but the key is to always start with the oral—either the teacher reads or recites a poem that students can easily understand, or a student, even if in another language, does so. To create a class poem, teachers can ask students for ideas or can use a topic that has come up in class that SLIFE found meaningful. Step-by-step, the class creates a poem, first brainstorming words related to the topic and then deciding how to put them together in a poem, playing with different forms of poetry and working with different rhythms and rhyme patterns. By searching "Reading Rockets" on the internet, you will find suggestions for creating poetry in the classroom. If you should choose to use these with SLIFE, remember to begin with the oral and not print, and to continually use the oral to scaffold the written.

Focus on Activities for Learning

SLIFE are used to learning what they need when they need it and developing skills through pragmatic, concrete tasks that have tangible results. Learning in formal education centers around literacy-based school tasks and underlying academic ways of thinking. When the students do not perform these school tasks successfully, it creates the impression that they are less intelligent and less able to engage in academics than other students (DeCapua & Triulzi, in press). Therefore, MALP® insists that teachers begin with familiar language and content to (1) foster familiarity and confidence in the academic ways of thinking by beginning with familiar language and content, and (2) promote skill in performing decontextualized tasks to demonstrate mastery (DeCapua & Marshall, 2011; Marshall & DeCapua, 2013).

Vocabulary level in an important consideration. At times, familiar language may be English that SLIFE have learned previously, but at other times, it is any language they know and want to use. Teachers should permit and encourage **translanguaging** in the classroom—that is, allow SLIFE to use any language they know in order to make teaching and learning comprehensible and accessible (Garcia et al., 2017; Garcia et al., 2013). By translanguaging, students are using their familiar languages as supports, not crutches, in learning a new language and developing new knowledge.

The key to focusing on activities for learning is to *not* introduce new material and new language at the same time as you are teaching SLIFE how to engage in a school task. In other words, if the task is new, be sure language and content are familiar. Recall the example regarding the concept of true/false questions. The students first practiced using contextualized information—familiar people and information—before moving to (from their perspective) decontextualized information and knowledge. Another illustration of beginning with familiar language and content to introduce and practice a decontextualized school task was the classification task from Ms. Zukowski's classroom where several suggestions were made as to how to prepare SLIFE to do the task by first using language and content they already knew.

The model in the Appendix shows the three components and six elements, three in each component.

5. Project-Based Learning

> Victor was placed in my beginner middle school ELL class. He had problems paying attention, knew only a little reading, writing, and was disengaged most of the time. I finally connected with him, and so did the other ELLs, when we did a poetry book project that compiled students' poems about something important to them.
>
> —A middle school teacher

The case for thinking in terms of projects instead of lessons when working with SLIFE has been made. Think about what you remember from school. What is likely to come to your mind is a project—perhaps the steaming volcano or salt map you created in science, or the student writing anthology from your English language arts class. Across the board, studies investigating culturally and linguistically diverse learners have found that project-based learning greatly enhances their learning experiences and educational outcomes (e.g., Boss & Krauss, 2018; Hammond, 2001; Honeyford, 2014; Sánchez et al., 2010; Walsh, 1999).

In a nutshell, project-based learning is hands-on, learner-centered learning that allows for differentiation, the incorporation of all the language skill areas (reading, writing, speaking, listening), and promotes the implementation of MALP® (DeCapua & Marshall, 2011; Marshall & DeCapua, 2009). Moreover, since teachers with SLIFE often find their students have a range of abilities, particularly if they are placed with other ELLs, project-based learning by nature allows for and accommodates differentiated instruction. In any project, there are tasks that can be geared to a variety of student interests and abilities. For example, a project may encompass tasks and activities including oral skills (e.g., interviews), writing (e.g., captions, summaries), visual skills (e.g. photos, posters), and publication (e.g., bulletin board displays, digital or printed booklets).

When it comes to SLIFE and project-based learning, several important points must be kept in mind:

- **Start small and keep it simple.** SLIFE are learning to do school. This includes learning how to work as a team on a project, understanding what tasks need to be accomplished and when they need to be accomplished by.

- **Introduce and practice classroom practices and procedures.** Don't assume familiarity with any or all of these, since another part of learning to do is school is becoming accustomed to standard practices and procedures.
- **Keep projects highly structured and recursive.** Structure and routine are important for SLIFE in learning to do school. Recursiveness is different than repetitiveness; project topics change but the types of projects and steps for implementation remain similar. Following the same general steps allows them to become automatic, decreasing the need for teachers to repeatedly spend valuable class time explaining and reviewing what students need to when, for widely differing project types.

Unsurprisingly, the first thing to keep in mind is Guideline #1, "Question your own assumptions." This means that when establishing the parameters for a project, avoid assuming that you think you know what will appeal to your SLIFE. Remember that what may be relevant from the perspective of a teacher, the text, or the curriculum may not have immediate relevance to SLIFE. For example, a project a teacher might think makes sense is on the topic of immigration. A common strategy is to begin with a published story of an immigrant's story. But for SLIFE who are on the left end of the Ways of Learning Continuum and thus new to print or with low-literacy skills, this is not necessarily a good way to introduce the topic. For them, they want to know who the person in the story is: who is Ahmed? Who is his family? I don't know Ahmed. Why do we read about him? Being able to engage in text removed from one's own lived experiences—an experience they have had—is part of becoming literate, but SLIFE may not be yet at that stage (DeCapua & Triulzi, in press). Even for SLIFE who are closer to the middle of the Ways of Learning Continuum, teachers need to ensure immediate relevance.

Regardless of where SLIFE are on the Ways of Learning Continuum, immediate relevance is always essential. To establish immediate relevance, intentionally follow Guideline #2, "Foster two-way communication." When there is such communication, teachers already either know their students' interests, abilities, or skills, or because of their relationship, can easily discover more and tap into possible funds of knowledge to use as the basis for selecting a project.

In terms of the immigration as a project then, rather than beginning with an unknown person's journey, begin with the students' own journeys. One way to do so can be through a survey. Students can ask each other questions such as:

- when they arrived
- where they first arrived
- what countries they traveled through or lived in before arriving
- with whom they came
- how they came.

[Note: Before engaging in such a survey and keeping in mind Guideline #2, teachers should know whether any of their students might be reluctant or uncomfortable sharing many details, particularly if they had traumatic journeys and/or entered without appropriate documents. Questions can be adjusted accordingly.]

These types of survey questions are immediately relevant and promote interconnectedness among SLIFE as they learn more about each other. Teachers should also participate in these surveys, either answering about themselves or about their ancestors so that SLIFE feel connected to them, too. In addition to providing an introduction to the selected project topic, survey questions provide rich data for use in support of Guideline #3, "Explicitly teach school tasks and academic ways of thinking." Tallying survey question responses and placing the results in a chart, for instance, is a school-based task.

Students asking each other when they came to this country promotes the learning of dates and how to say and write them. On the one hand, this is a language learning activity as they learn to say the dates in English; on the other hand, looking at and discussing their responses has students practice the academic task of organizing and sequencing time. SLIFE may come from backgrounds that did not place a high priority on dates and, in some cases, may not be sure of their date of birth (they may have had one legally assigned to them for preparation of immigration or refugee documents). Identifying and comparing where students entered the country, what countries they traveled from and through, and where they live now can become the basis for working on mapping and geography skills.

These are only a few ideas of how surveys not only provide an introduction to a particular topic, but how the data they generate can serve to promote language, content, and academic ways of thinking. DeCapua and Marshall (2011) provide an extended discussion on constructing survey questions and using class surveys as the foundation for projects. For examples of surveys to introduce a variety of projects, see also DeCapua and colleagues (in press) and Marshall & DeCapua (2013; 2018).

Another highly effective strategy for ensuring that a project is immediately relevant to your SLIFE is to use the Language Experience Approach (LEA). After the class has shared an experience, it becomes the basis of a jointly created text. This experience can be anything from listening to a story to watching a video to going on a field trip or planting a garden. The jointly created written text traditionally becomes the focus of a variety of literacy activities. In addition, this text can lead into a variety of different projects that go beyond the focus on literacy. These can include such projects as producing a book featuring students' personal stories; maintaining a log or journal recording events to use for creating charts, table, and graphs; or creating informational leaflets, brochures, posters, or slide presentations.

DeCapua and Marshall (2011) and Marshall and DeCapua (2013) provide a detailed overview and extended examples of the steps in a project. To summarize, these are:

1. **Brainstorm possible project ideas**. Although initially brainstorming may not be realistic and teachers will need to provide ideas based on what they know about their students, at some point teachers should carefully involve the students in generating topic ideas. Let's consider weather as an example. In areas with harsh winters, SLIFE may not be familiar with the necessary clothing. Rather than telling them what they need to wear or asking them to fill out worksheets about weather and clothing, there are many ideas that lend themselves to projects. Start, for instance, with a collection of assorted clothing items such as hats, gloves, scarves, jackets, and boots. These can be collected by the teacher or the school community.
2. **Select a focus.** Topics need to be realistic and projects in line with these key points:
   - **Start small and keep it simple.** What can be accomplished realistically? Remember that less is better. Consider the projected time frame, student schedules, and how many of the practices and procedures will be new or relatively unfamiliar to the SLIFE. Using the clothing collection, what projects might grow out of this? One might be a store where SLIFE and even other students could buy gently used clothing. While this may seem like a useful

and practical project, realistically it would require a great deal of time, planning, and organization and therefore not be an appropriate project, at least initially. Instead, the teacher might consider taking a selection of the items, putting a price tag on each one, and allotting each student a certain sum of play money. The students then decide which items they need and which ones they can afford to buy. They can prepare posters or leaflets with the items and their costs that show or describe which items one needs for what reason. In this sample project, students can practice vocabulary, math, and cause and effect in the sense of how weather and temperature affect the human body.

- **Introduce and practice classroom practices and procedures.** Which ones will be new or different? Students may be used to sharing responsibilities, but are they used to working formally in small groups, each person with an assigned task? How will students be kept on task and on schedule? Displaying a large calendar with due dates and consistently reviewing these is one technique. Another is having a posted checklist with what needs to be done by whom and when.
- **Keep projects highly structured and recursive**. One way to think of projects is to think in terms of Russian *Matryoshka* nesting dolls, whereby wooden dolls of decreasing size are placed inside one another. Likewise, small projects lead to increasingly bigger, more complex ones. A simple immigration survey might lead to a geography project in which students describe and map their journeys. Another survey on students' immigration experiences might lead to a project comparing historical changes in immigration patterns, which in turn could lead to a book project on stories by the SLIFE on their immigration experiences.

3. **Identify tasks, skills, and materials required**. What needs to be done and who has which skills? How can all SLIFE be involved allowing for different language proficiencies and literacy skills? Are there any particularly artistic or creative students? Are there any specialized materials required? Will students need, for instance, to learn how to use any new technology before some part of the project can be undertaken?
4. **Delegate specific tasks**. Not all tasks need to be delegated at the beginning. As a project develops, additional tasks will be identified

and can be assigned at that time. Tasks can be also be rotated among students.

5. **Implement the project.** This is the core of the experience in which SLIFE develop language skills and practice academic ways of thinking underlying decontextualized school tasks. Depending on the type of project, this is also where SLIFE build subject-area content knowledge. At the same time, teachers ensure that all elements of MALP® are addressed over the course of the project.
6. **Share the project**. Sharing completed projects whether virtually or in real time with fellow students, the larger school community, and/or family members provides SLIFE with an added sense of accomplishment when they showcase their efforts.
7. **Reflect and evaluate the project.** This can be as simple as eliciting a thumbs up or down about what students liked or did not like. For more proficient students, teachers can ask more complex questions such as, "What should we do differently next time?" In their reflection and discussion, the class can also consider what other ideas for different projects arose as they worked on the project, thereby starting the cycle with #1 again.

Sample Project Incorporating MALP®

To help teachers in implementing this culturally responsive instructional model, use the MALP® Teacher Planning Checklist in the Appendix. This Checklist mirrors the three components of MALP® and is intended to help you plan, as well as evaluate, incorporation of all six elements (see Figure 4.1). It is not sufficient to include one, two, or even four or five elements; all six must be present and if not in a single lesson, then over the course of a series of lessons or a project.

Let's now examine how one teacher, Ms. Cole, engaged in her students in her Neighborhoods Project while incorporating MALP® (Cole & Elson, 2014; Cole et al., 2015). The SLIFE, from a variety of different countries, had very low literacy skills. Working together, they created a class booklet describing the different students' neighborhoods. The class decided to work on neighborhoods because of student interest in learning more about where they all live. This topic provided a wealth of immediately relevant subject matter, including in which stores they shop, which buses they take, and what resources, such as a park, they have access to in their neighborhood. Ms. Cole planned the steps for this class project using the MALP® Checklist (see the Appendix).

Step 1

The project began with a general discussion of the concept of neighborhoods. The students discussed informally where in Pittsburgh (or just outside the city), they lived. Students practiced orally asking and answering using sentence frames:

Where do you live?	I live in Pittsburgh.
My neighborhood is ____.	My neighborhood is Troy Hill.

The students and the teacher developed interconnectedness through sharing about themselves and where they live. More proficient students wrote neighborhood names on the board with spelling help from the other students and the instructor. All the students helped with the spelling on the board, thereby scaffolding the written through the oral, and sharing the responsibility of spelling.

Step 2

Students learned and practiced vocabulary for talking about their neighborhoods. Ms. Cole provided color photos from the internet plus others she took in the students' neighborhoods to illustrate typical neighborhood landmarks, such as *bank*, *drugstore*, and *park*. The students practiced saying the words while looking at the photos. After the students had mastered the words orally, they matched the photos with index cards of the printed, corresponding word—that is, placing an index card with the word *bank* on the color photo of a bank. Matching is an example of a decontextualized school-based task.

Step 3

Once the students were comfortable with naming the place or object and with reading some of the words on index cards, the class played games with the photo and word cards. One of the most popular of these was Flyswatter, in which the students played on teams to swat the photo corresponding to the word Ms. Cole read aloud. In alignment with MALP®, the students capitalized on their oral skills and familiarity with the subject matter to scaffold and support use of print.

Step 4

After the students had learned the neighborhood vocabulary orally and could read the one-word cards, Ms. Cole introduced a short model text describing her neighborhood. The students first listened and then listened again and repeated as a group as she pointed to each word; this built connections between the oral and the written. Later, students received a copy of the text and practiced reading it aloud with a partner.

Once the students understood the model text, they practiced asking and answering simple questions about it to demonstrate their ability to use the information in the text to answer questions, such as "Is there a _____ (bank) in the teacher's neighborhood?" This activity began to prepare students for comprehension and the more complex critical reading questions.

Step 5

Using Ms. Cole's text as a model, the students began preparing sentences about their own neighborhoods. Ms. Cole differentiated the activity based on student abilities. Students with low literacy provided their sentences orally, which she recorded and transcribed for them. Students with somewhat stronger literacy skills completed a cloze sheet or simple sentence frames to describe their own neighborhoods:

I live in ________________________
In my neighborhood, I ____________.
In my neighborhood, there _________.
I like _________________________.
I don't like ______________________.

Subsequently, Ms. Cole typed up the students' descriptions, which they then compiled into a booklet. Students were also tasked with taking a photo of something they liked in their neighborhood to include with their descriptive text.

Step 6

These student-created booklets formed the basis for additional literacy activities. For one, Ms. Cole identified key words from the students' stories and had the students sort the words according to first letter (or first two letters in some cases) consonant sounds. Activities such as these encourage phonemic and phonic awareness, which is essential in emergent literacy. Second, the students practiced syntax by reconstructing simple sentences from each other's stories using large, cut-up versions of sentences from the stories. In addition, students practiced an academic way of thinking, namely comparison and contrast, by examining each other's stories to find the similarities and differences in their various neighborhoods. Finally, by becoming authors themselves, the students became more connected to the world of print and how it related to their more familiar real world outside the classroom.

The Neighborhoods Project clearly accepted conditions essential to learning in that the subject matter was **immediately relevant** to the students' lives. These were not imaginary, decontextualized neighborhoods and vocabulary in a text, but their own neighborhoods. In seeing photos and speaking, reading, and writing about their neighborhoods, the students learned about each other, discovering that many of them lived close to each other and shopped in the same stores. This served to promote **interconnectedness** and a sense of community among the students. During the course of the project, we see that the processes for learning were combined: the students had ample opportunities to **share responsibility,** yet they also had to demonstrate **individual accountability.** They worked together to develop their stories and create the class Neighborhoods booklet, yet each student was in charge of his or her own story. The students were also given the opportunity for shared responsibility by repeating chorally and reading in partnership. Ms. Cole also carefully **combined the oral with the written** by engaging in such activities as choral reading, while pointing to individual words and games that required simultaneous attention to both the oral and written. Also central to this project was Ms. Cole's focus on **developing students' academic ways of thinking by using familiar language and content** as they learned to **engage in decontextualized tasks.** For example, students had to match, compare and contrast, and answer, and later come up with, text-based questions. The Neighborhoods Project leveraged students' strengths and interests to make decontextualized tasks more accessible and grounded in material and delivery method already comfortable and familiar to them.

Final Reflection

The goal of this ebook was to help you understand more about SLIFE and to present some suggestions as to how to help them in the classroom. Underlying this is the belief that we must work together to avoid the all-too-prevalent deficit perspective, a result of evaluating SLIFE through our lens of formal education and judging them as lacking. If, instead, we accept that SLIFE have come to our classrooms with significantly different prior learning experiences and knowledge and skills, we can recognize that they bring much to our classrooms and that it is our job as teachers to learn what they bring and to actively incorporate it into our teaching. This also results in our being better able to adapt and modify our teaching to transition SLIFE to the demands and expectations of formal education and in reducing the cultural dissonance they face as they navigate the unfamiliar and strange world of formal education. Instrumental in working together with SLIFE to do so is following the four Guidelines as discussed throughout this ebook:

Guideline #1: Question your own assumptions.
Guideline #2: Foster two-way communication.
Guideline #3: Explicitly teach school tasks and academic ways of thinking.
Guideline #4: Promote project-based learning.

Furthermore, in transitioning SLIFE to formal education, teachers must strive to consistently implement the MALP® instructional model (see the Appendix).

MALP® Teacher Planning Checklist

Mutually Adaptive Learning Paradigm®

A. Accept Conditions for Learning
A1. I am making this lesson/project immediately relevant to my students' lives. Explain:
A2. I am helping students develop and maintain interconnectedness with each other. Explain:
B. Combine Processes for Learning
B1. I am incorporating both shared responsibility and individual accountability. Explain:
B2. I am scaffolding the written word through oral interaction. Explain:
C. Focus on New Activities for Learning
C1. I am developing academic ways of thinking. Explain:
C2. I am teaching students to engage in decontextualized tasks to demonstrate mastery. Explain:
C3. I am using familiar language and content as scaffolds. Explain:

REFERENCES

Altherr Flores, J. A. (2017). Social semiotics and multimodal assessment of L2 adult emergent readers from refugee backgrounds. In M. Sosiński (Ed.). *Alfabetación y aprendizaje de idiomas por adultos: Investigación, política educativa y práctica docente (Literacy education and second language learning by adults: Research, policy and practice* (pp.9–31). *Proceedings of the 2016 LESLLA Symposium*, Granada, Spain: Universidad de Granada.

Ardila, A., Bertolucci, P., Braga, L. Castro-Caldas, A., Judd, T., Kosmidis, M., Matute, E., Nitrini, R., Ostrosky-Solis F., & Rosselli, M. (2010). Illiteracy: The neuropsychology of cognition without reading. *Archives of Clinical Neuropsychology, 25*, 689–712.

Asher, J. (1982). *Learning another language through actions: The complete teacher's guidebook.* Los Gatos, CA: Sky Oaks Productions.

Bigelow, M., & Watson, J. (2012). The role of educational level, literacy, and orality in L2 learning. In S. Gass & A. Mackey (Eds.). *The Routledge handbook of second language acquisition* (pp. 461–475). New York: Routledge.

Boss, S., & Krauss, J. (2018). *Reinventing project- based learning: Your field guide to real-world projects in the digital age* (3rd ed.). International Society for Technology in Education (ISTE).

Bow Valley College. (2009). *Learning for life: An ESL literacy handbook.* Available at: https://globalaccess.bowvalleycollege.ca/products-services/practical-guide-teaching-esl-literacy

Browder, C. (2018). Recently resettled refugee students learning English in U.S. high schools: The impact of students' educational backgrounds. In T. Shapiro, R. Farrely, and M. Curry (Eds.), *Educating refugee-background students: Critical Issues and Dynamic Contexts.* Bristol, UK: Multilingual Matters.

Bruer, J. T. (1993). *Schools for thought: A science of learning in the classroom.* Cambridge, MA: MIT Press.

Burt, M., Peyton, J. K., & Adams, R. (2003). *Reading and adult English language learners: A review of the research.* Washington, DC: Center for Applied Linguistics. Retrieved from http://www.cal.org/caela/research/RAELL.pdf

Cole, S. M. & Elson, A. (2014). Implementing the Mutually Adaptive Learning Paradigm in the LESLLA classroom. In I. van de Craats, J. Kuvers, & R. Van Hout (Eds.). *Adult literacy, second language and cognition* (pp. 199–126). Nijmegen, the Netherlands: Center for Language Studies (CLS). Retrieved from https://drive.google.com/drive/folders/1bAQ377KFMHrfsfTZBgyNCd-8nJecvoWw

Cole, S., Marshall, H.W., & Murphy, K. (2015). Implementing the Mutually Adaptive Learning Paradigm in a community-based program. Presentation at the 2015 annual LESLLA (Literacy Education and Second Language Learning for Adults) Symposium, Flagler College, St. Augustine, FL.

DeCapua, A. (2016). Reaching students with limited or interrupted formal education: A culturally responsive approach. *Language and Linguistics Compass, 10,* 225–237.

DeCapua, A. (2017). *Grammar for teachers: A guide to American English for native and non-native speakers of English* (2nd ed.). New York: Springer.

DeCapua, A. (2018a). *Culture myths: Applying second language research to classroom teaching.* Ann Arbor: University of Michigan.

DeCapua, A. (2018b). Students with limited or interrupted formal education (SLIFE). In J. Govoni (Ed.). *Preparing the way: Teaching ELs in the pre-K–12 classroom* (pp. 63–87). Dubuque, IA: Kendall Hunt.

DeCapua, A., & Marshall, H. W. (2010). Limited formally schooled English language learners in U.S. classrooms. *Urban Review, 42,* 159–173.

DeCapua, A., & Marshall, H. W. (2011). *Breaking new ground: Teaching students with limited or interrupted formal education in U.S. secondary schools.* Ann Arbor: University of Michigan Press.

DeCapua, A., & Marshall, H. W. (2013). Making the transition to classroom success: Culturally responsive teaching for struggling language learners. Ann Arbor: University of Michigan Press.

DeCapua, A. & Triulzi, M. (in press). Learning for work: Hidden challenges for LESLLA learners. To appear in the 2018 Proceedings of the annual LESLLA Symposium, Palermo, Italy.

DeCapua, A., & Wintergerst, A. (2016). *Crossing cultures in the language classroom.* (2nd ed.). Ann Arbor: University of Michigan Press.

DeCapua, A., Marshall, H. W., & Tang, F. L. (in press). *Meeting the needs of students with limited or interrupted formal education (SLIFE)* (2nd ed.). Ann Arbor: University of Michigan Press.

DeCapua, A., Smathers, W., & Tang, F. (2009). *Meeting the needs of students with limited or interrupted schooling (SLIFE)*. Ann Arbor: University of Michigan Press.

Echevarria, J., Vogt, M. E., & Short, D. (2016). *Making content comprehensible for English learners: The SIOP model* (5th ed.). White Plains, NY: Pearson.

Finnegan R. (2017). *Oral poetry: Its nature, significance and social context* (2nd ed.). Eugene, OR: Wipf and Stock.

Flaitz, J. (2018). *Refugee students: What every ESL teacher needs to know.* Ann Arbor: University of Michigan Press.

Flynn, J. (2007). *What is intelligence?* New York: Cambridge University Press.

Freeman, Y., & Freeman, S. (2002). *Closing the achievement gap: How to reach limited-formal-schooling and long-term English learners.* Portsmouth, NH: Heinemann.

García, O., Lin, A. M. Y., & May, S. (2017). *Bilingual and multilingual education.* New York: Springer International Publishing

García, O., Woodley, H. H., Flores, N., & Chu, H. (2013). Latino emergent bilingual youth in high schools: Transcaring strategies for academic success. *Urban Education, 48*(6), 798–827.

Gay, G. (2000) *Culturally responsive teaching: Theory, research and practice.* New York: Teachers College Press.

Gay, G. (2018). *Culturally responsive teaching: Theory, research and practice* (3rd ed.). New York: Teachers College Press.

González, N., Moll, L. C., & Amanti, C. (Eds.). (2005). *Funds of knowledge: Theorizing practices in households, communities, and classrooms.* Mahwah, NJ: Lawrence Erlbaum.

Grabe, W. & Stoller, F. (2011). *Teaching and researching reading* (2nd ed.). New York: Routledge.

Grigorenko, E. (2007). Hitting, missing, and in between: A typology of the impact of western education on the non-western world. *Comparative Education, 43*, 165–186.

Hammond, L. (2001). Notes from California: An anthropological approach to urban science education for language minority families. *Journal of Research in Science Teaching, 38*, 983–999.

Hofstede, G., & Hofstede, G. J. (2005). *Cultures and organizations: Software of the mind* (2nd ed.). New York: McGraw-Hill.

Honeyford, M. A. (2014). From aquí and allá. *Journal of Literacy Research, 46*, 194–233.

Honigsfeld, A. & Dove, M. (2014). *Co-teaching for English learners: A guide to collaborative planning, instruction, assessment, and reflections*. Thousand Oaks, CA: Corwin.

Kurvers, J. (2015). Emerging literacy in adult second-language learners: A synthesis of research findings in the Netherlands. *Writing Systems Research*, 7, 58–78.

Luria, A. R. (1976). *The making of mind*. Cambridge, MA: Harvard University Press.

MacDonald, M. R. (Ed.). (1999). *Traditional storytelling today: An international sourcebook*. New York: Routledge.

Marshall, H. W. (1998). A mutually adaptive learning paradigm for Hmong students. *Cultural Circles*, 3, 135–149.

Marshall, H. W. & DeCapua, A. (2009). The newcomer booklet: A project for limited formally schooled students. *ELT Journal*, 64, 396–404.

Marshall, H. W. & DeCapua, A. (2013). *Making the transition to classroom success: Culturally responsive teaching for struggling language learners*. Ann Arbor: University of Michigan Press.

Marshall, H. W. & DeCapua, A. (2018, April). Promoting achievement for struggling ESL students: Five recommendations. *Secondary Accents*, TESOL International Association.

Meltzer, J., Smith, N., & Clark, H. (2002). *Adolescent literacy resources: Linking research and practice*. Providence, RI: Northeast and Islands Regional Educational Laboratory at Brown University. Retrieved from: https://www.govinfo.gov/content/pkg/ERIC-ED466788/pdf/ERIC-ED466788.pdf

Nessel, D., & Dixon, C. (2008). *Using the Language Experience Approach with English language learners: Strategies for engaging students and developing literacy*. Thousand Oaks, CA: Corwin.

Ngo, B. (2010). Doing "diversity" at Dynamic High: Problems and possibilities of multicultural education in practice. *Education and Urban Society*, 42, 473–495.

Robinson, K. (2011). *Out of our minds: Learning to be creative*. New York: John Wiley.

Ruiz-de-Velasco, J., & Fix, M. (2000). *Overlooked and underserved: Immigrant students in U.S. secondary schools*. Urban Institute. Available at: https://eric.ed.gov/?id=ED44927

Sánchez, C., Plata, V., Grosso, L., & Leird, B. (2010). Encouraging Spanish-speaking families' involvement through Dichos. *Journal of Latinos and Education*, 9, 239–248.

Savina, E., Garrity, K., Kenny, P. & Doerr, C. (2016). The benefits of movement for youth: A whole child approach. *Contemporary School Psychology, 20*, 282–292.

Silva, K. G., Correa-Chávez, M., & Rogoff, B. (2010) Mexican-heritage children's attention and learning from interactions directed to others. *Child Development, 81*, 898–912.

Snow, A. M. & Brinton, D. (2017). *The content-based classroom: New perspectives on integrating language and content* (2nd ed.). Ann Arbor: University of Michigan Press.

Strauss, V. (October 24, 2014). Teacher spends two days as a student and is shocked at what she learns. *Washington Post.* Retrieved from https://www.washingtonpost.com/news/answer-sheet/wp/2014/10/24/teacher-spends-two-days-as-a-student-and-is-shocked-at-what-she-learned/?utm_term=.0d6b39ddc83b

Tarone E., Bigelow, M. & Hansen, K. (2007). The impact of alphabetic print literacy on oral second language acquisition. In N. Faux (Ed.). *Low-educated second language and literacy acquisition: Research, policy, and practice: Proceedings of the 2nd annual forum* (pp. 22–43). Richmond, VA. The Literacy Institute at Virginia Commonwealth University.

Treschan, L., & Mehrotra, A. (2013). *Young Mexican Americans in New York City: Working more and earning less.* New York: Community Service Society. UNICEF.

Triandis, H. C. (1995). *Individualism and collectivism.* Boulder, CO: Westview Press.

Walqui, A. & van Lier, L. (2010). *Scaffolding the academic success of adolescent English language learners: A pedagogy of promise.* San Francisco, CA: WestEd.

Walsh, C. (1999). Enabling academic success for secondary students with limited formal schooling: A study of the Haitian literacy program at Hyde Park High School in Boston. The Education Alliance, LAB at Brown University. Retrieved from https://www.brown.edu/academics/education-alliance/sites/brown.edu.academics.education-alliance/files/publications/HaitianLit.pdf

Williams, A., & Chapman, L. (2007). Meeting diverse needs; content-based language teaching and settlement needs for low literacy adult ESL immigrants. In M. Young-Scholten (Ed.). *Low-educated adult second language and literacy acquisition: Proceedings of the Third Annual Forum* (pp. 49–60). Newcastle-upon-Tyne, UK: Newcastle University.